ABBÉ R

How to Read the Bible

✠ ✠ ✠

Translated by a Nun of
REGINA LAUDIS, O.S.B.

Sophia Institute Press®
Manchester, NH

Sophia Institute Press®
Box 5284, Manchester, NH 03108
1-800-888-9344
www.SophiaInstitute.com

Cover design by Theodore Schluenderfritz.

Image: St. Matthew by El Greco, Indianapolis Museum of Art, USA/
The Clowes Fund Collection/ The Bridgeman Art Library.

Printed in the United States of America.

This translation is made from the second edition of *Ouvrons
la Bible* (Paris-Brussels, Editions Universitaires, 1950). Originally
published in 1953 by P.J. Kenedy & Sons, New York.

Nihil Obstat: Rev. Leonard A. Bushinski, C.S.Sp. *Censor Deputatis.*
Imprimatur: Most Reverend Henry J. O'Brien, D.D.
Bishop of Hartford, February 23, 1953.

Library of Congress Cataloging-in-Publication Data

Poelman, Roger, 1911-
  [Ouvrons la Bible. English]
  How to read the Bible / Roger Poelman ; translated by
a Nun of Regina Laudis.
    p. cm.
  Originally published: New York : P. J. Kenedy & Sons, 1953.
  Includes bibliographical references and index.
  ISBN 978-1-933184-66-1 (ppbk : alk. paper) 1. Bible—Reading.
2. Bible—Outlines, syllabi, etc. I. Title.
  BS617.P614 2010
  220.07—dc22

                                    2009037193

How to Read the Bible

Editor's Note

THIS is a fairly free but wholly faithful translation of Abbé Poelman's guide to the Bible, *Ouvrons la Bible* (Let's Open the Bible). In the interest of precision the title has been changed for American readers, but we have preserved the author's approach and spirit—that of *first opening* and *establishing contact* with the Holy Bible.

In the matter of Scriptural references, clarity rather than consistency of publishing style has been the rule. There are standard abbreviations for the books of the Bible, but we have used them only when the reference is perfectly clear or very well known. Almost all of us know that "Matt." stands for the Gospel According to St. Matthew, and that "Cor." with a "I" or "II" before it means St. Paul's First or Second Epistle to the Corinthians. But some of the less obvious ones we have written out—at least the first few times.

After a little practice you will see at a glance that

the Roman numeral before the name of the book tells which of the books of the same name is referred to. The first Arabic numeral after the name of the book designates the chapter, and the Arabic numeral after the colon (:) designates the verse or verses. Thus:

> I Kings 1 means the first chapter of the first Book of Kings.
>
> Galatians (or Gal.) 3 means the whole third chapter of St. Paul's Epistle to the Galatians.
>
> Genesis (or Gen.) 28:10 means the tenth verse of the 28th chapter of the Book of Genesis.
>
> Genesis 28:10–22 means the passage beginning with the tenth and ending with the 22nd verse of the 28th chapter of the Book of Genesis.

Though in this country we usually do not divide the Book of Isaias, with the section from Chapter 40 to Chapter 66 designated as the Book of Consolation, there is sound critical basis for this division, as will be realized when we follow the Old Testament narrative. Also, with Abbé Poelman, we have preserved the Hebrew names for the first and second Book of Samuel (I and II Kings) and the first and second Paralipomenon (I and II Chronicles). The Douay-Rheims translation of the Latin Vulgate has been used in all Scriptural quotations.

Author's Preface

THE TEXT of this second edition has been revised and corrected.

In line with the criticisms received, we have amplified the notes on the Gospel of St. Luke and given a more important place to St. Mark.

We have inverted the position of the prophets Osee and Amos, and placed the Book of Consolation (chapters 40–66 of Isaias) after Ezechiel.

A few historical references have been retouched.

In other respects the book retains its simplicity and brevity, which are intended to make it easier for the reader to follow the unfolding of the essentials of theology in the Scriptures. Our various critics tell us that guidance in this direction is the most useful service we have rendered in these pages.

> Wherefore having the loins of your mind girt up, being sober, trust perfectly in the grace which is offered you in the revelation of Jesus Christ (I Pet. 1:13).

R. P.

Contents

CONTENTS

x

Introduction

THIS is a small book, but it has a great message for you: *God has spoken to us.* That God should have spoken is an event of greater importance than all earthly adventures put together. And the Bible brings us God's message.

The paragraphs of this little manual are like so many bookmarks for the pages of your Bible; their chief ambition is to show you what sections best reveal the plot of the only book that counts.

The Bible pertains to the history of the human race, yet it is not a history book like those we studied in school. It tells us what God wanted us to know about Him: how we were created by love and redeemed by love. He makes Himself known as a Father talking to His children in words they can understand. The whole human race is His child; as the child begins to grow up, the Father's words become more profound.

Because the essential thing in the Bible is this message of God, which has come down to us changeless through the centuries, expressed partly in words and partly in doings that somehow hint of God's hidden plan, the author has not stressed any facts connected with history, science, or geography. He wants the keystone of the arch to stand out in full view.

We recommend this book to you, therefore, as a guide to the Bible, and we place it under the patronage of the Queen of heaven and earth.

CANON LUCIEN CERFAUX

The University of Louvain

CHAPTER 1

Contacting the Bible

✠　✠　✠

WHAT is our religion? This question can be answered in two words: Jesus Christ.

Explicit faith in Jesus Christ, the Lord and Son of God, distinguishes Christianity from all other religions and philosophies.

Do you believe that Jesus is Christ the Lord, the Son of God? This is the basic question put to the first Christians, and we too must answer it. Do you believe in Christ? Do you know Christ? Do you believe in Him and know Him not merely in a vague, indefinite way, but by direct contact with Him and acceptance of His teaching? Who can fail to catch the enthusiasm in these words of John the Apostle:

> That which was from the beginning, which we
> have heard, which we have seen with our eyes, which
> we have looked upon, and our hands have handled,
> of the word of life: for the life was manifested; and

I

we have seen and do bear witness, and declare unto you the life eternal, which was with the Father, and hath appeared to us: that which we have seen and have heard, we declare unto you, that you also may have fellowship with us, and our fellowship may be with the Father, and with His Son Jesus Christ. And these things we write to you, that you may rejoice, and your joy may be full (I John 1:1–4).

This passage seems to us to give an exact idea of what the Catholic does when he opens the Bible. He finds the most important of all tidings—that the life eternal, which was with the Father, has appeared; and this makes him eager to see, handle, and hear the Word of Life, so that he may have fellowship with Him.

We shall start with the Gospel, which is the loftiest, most sacred, and most mysterious part of the whole Bible. Here, in Christ, is revealed that inmost life of God which is the source of the joy promised to us.

From this summit we shall set out on a course that will lead us through the books of the Old and the New Testament, so that we may be able to comprehend with all the saints the breadth and length and height and depth of God's love, and thus arrive at a fuller knowledge of the hope to which we have been called and the riches of our glory.

Many people hear the Bible talked about, and

perhaps they read books and articles about it; but few Catholics open the book itself. And if some one should open it, what is he to look for? Anyone who does not know the landmarks and the road through the Scriptures will soon feel like a traveler lost in the jungle.

It is our wish to help the Catholic reader in his first contacts with the Bible, point out the key chapters, and show him how to read them according to the unfolding of revelation, deposited in the Church and guaranteed to us by her.

✠

THE FIRST CONTACT: ST. LUKE

THE GOOD tidings shed their light on the pages of both Testaments; so let us come at once to the Gospel.

We are now opening one of the three synoptics, St. Luke.[1] Luke writes with a kind of joyfulness which is characteristically Christian. He intended his book for the Gentiles (among whom most of us are included), wishing to show them in what way and to what extent Christ is the Saviour of the world.

---

[1] The name synoptic, which means "taking a common view," is applied to the first three Gospels because of their many similarities in plan, approach, and content.—*Translator's note.*

3

"Saviour of the world"—we must give more thought to these words. Dante observed that St. Luke is the historian of Christ's gentleness. Historian, and a competent one, St. Luke consulted the various sources within his reach and wrote a connected account of the events relating to Jesus. He takes care to tell us so in his Prologue (1:1–4).

His history begins with the accounts of Christ's infancy, where we meet two important characters —that mighty saint, John the Baptist, and our Lady with her surpassing purity and holiness. We can hardly be too grateful that St. Luke has given us not only the account of the annunciation and Christ's birth at Bethlehem, but also the four canticles that the Church has incorporated into her liturgy (1:5—2:52).

The first part of the Gospel tells the story of Christ's preaching in Galilee, and here St. Luke often draws upon the tradition of St. Matthew and St. Mark. Two passages particularly are found in Luke alone—the raising to life of the son of the widow of Naim (7:11–17) and the conversion of the sinful woman (7:36–50).

The second part is more clearly stamped by St. Luke's special genius (chapters 9 through 24). These chapters give us a moral and religious character sketch of Christ. The main themes of this section are the goodness of Christ and joy that salvation is brought to all men.

4

Read the parables carefully, especially the parable of the good Samaritan (10:25–37); the three parables of divine mercy—the lost sheep, the lost groat and the prodigal son (chapter 15); and the parable of the Pharisee and the Publican (18:9–14).

Chapter 24 has a charm all its own, as it recaptures the atmosphere of the first Easter with such freshness and finesse. The central story of the disciples of Emmaus—like a parable of the wayfaring Church—seems, in the simplicity of its telling, to give forth rays of light, joy, and certainty.

It is a good plan to reread the text of this Gospel in large sections.

The subtitles in the Bible will prove extremely useful. They will help us to penetrate into the spirit of the good tidings, making the figure of Christ stand out more clearly and at the same time more delicately etched.

Thus our Lord is presented to us, and our first contact with Him has been made.

✠

THE FULL LIGHT: ST. JOHN

Now if we wish to have full light by which to penetrate into the Holy Scriptures, we must pause again at their climax, namely chapters 13 through 17 of St. John, and read them attentively.

We may take these chapters as an immediate preparation for our reading of the Bible.

In this discourse Christ imparts to us the life-giving knowledge of theology, which is the secret of God's inmost life. Now we shall be able to take a truly Christian view of the divine Economy in all its length and breadth, and follow stage by stage its different manifestations.

"O foolish, and slow of heart to believe in all things which the prophets have spoken. Ought not Christ to have suffered these things, and so to enter into His glory?" *And beginning at Moses and all the prophets,* He expounded to them in all the scriptures, the things that were concerning Him (Luke 24:25–27).

CHAPTER 2

In the Beginning

✠ ✠ ✠

GENESIS

THE FIRST chapters of Genesis give in two successive accounts a simple, graphic answer to the grave questions with which every human being is confronted.

God is shown to be the One from whom all things derive their origin. Nothing is evil, whether matter or spirit. The cosmos is presented as having a sacred meaning, and man appears as a keystone in it.

Man is made to the image and likeness of God Himself. In order to understand man, we must look at Christ, "the image of the invisible God, the firstborn of every creature" (Col. 1:15). Now "we all beholding the glory of the Lord with open face, are transformed into the same image from glory to glory, as by the Spirit of the Lord" (II Cor. 3:18).

The second discovery in these first chapters is

that of freedom, and, unfortunately, of sin. Man had been given this freedom so that he might love God and fling himself into His arms. Punishment cut short the illusion that a paradise might some day be regained on earth, and laid bare disorder and evil.

But that disaster was far from being the end of the story. The light of this initial revelation shone out in the protogospel:[1] "I will put enmities between thee (the serpent) and the woman, and thy seed and her seed: she shall crush thy head, and thou shalt lie in wait for her heel" (Gen. 3:15). This passage alludes to the Messias—to Christ the new Adam and Mary the new Eve. Everything came from God; everything was good. Then at the very start harm was done by man's fall. But everything was to be restored (restored to life, raised from the dead) by the Saviour.

> Therefore, as by the offence of one, unto all men to condemnation; so also by the justice of One, unto all men to justification of life. For as by the disobedience of one man, many were made sinners; so also by the obedience of One, many shall be made just (Rom. 5:18–19).

This passage shows us the wide implications of the very first pages of our Bible reading. The light of Christ has already reached them.

---

[1] Protogospel or protevangelium is the name given to this verse of Genesis as being the first announcement of the coming of a Saviour.—*Translator's note.*

Read GENESIS 1–3.

We know God the Creator; He is the Father of our Lord Jesus Christ. Let us see Him at work "in the beginning" in the Prologue of John's Gospel (John 1:1–18).[2]

In Job 38:1—40:5, God voices His lordship over creation in poetic and striking terms.

The revelation of nature as the work of God's hands is sumptuously reviewed in some of the psalms, where it serves as an object of prayer, contemplation and praise. Read, for instance, Psalms 8, 138, and, in particular, 103.[3]

(Note: We shall often bring in psalms as we make these first contacts with the Bible. This will give us opportunities to form the habit of using the psalms as an expression of our own feelings toward God, and as part of our own prayer.)

The creation of man in particular is set forth in the "wisdom" literature, Ecclesiasticus 17:1—18:13.

✠

FROM the prehistory of the people of God, there emerge two names—Abel and Noe—and the picture of the tower of Babel.

---

[2] As we take up the key chapters, we shall refer to other Biblical passages which throw fuller light on them. The reader who follows out this scheme will soon have a certain grasp of the Bible and be able to find his way easily through the maze of books.

[3] The numbers refer to the Vulgate.

Abel and Cain stand together on the threshold of human adventures, as the representative good man and evil man. Abel's story offers us the first ritual notion of sacrifice to God, and the death that befell him, despite his innocence, shows us the results of sin.

With Noe comes the story of the flood and the new beginning effected by God. A sacrifice of thanksgiving inaugurated the new era, and the all-important notion of the covenant was outlined for the first time when God said to Noe: "Behold I will establish My covenant with you" (Gen. 9:9). This covenant was handed on to Sem. Christ was to be a Semite.

The tower of Babel ended with the confusion of tongues and the scattering abroad of mankind; this is balanced in the New Testament by the unity regained on the first Pentecost (Gen. 11:1–9 and Acts 2:1–12).

CHAPTER 3

The Three Patriarchs

✠ ✠ ✠

ABRAHAM

AFTER the first eleven chapters of Genesis, a great turning point in the religious history of men is discernible; it is the call of God to Abraham. From the old decaying trunk of the human race, God broke off a frail branch which He bore away by the breath of the Spirit and planted in a land marked out by Himself—the promised land.

Many a trial, many a purification, and many a promise were the milestones of Abraham's spiritual journey by that upward pathway which was to shape the future destinies of our souls. God found in Abraham a man ready to answer His call with heroic faith. At the moment when Abraham was invited to go forth out of his country and from his kindred and out of his father's house, the land of Chanaan became the promised land. Abraham was to dwell all the days of his life in this land of

Chanaan as a stranger and a foreigner. Moving from camp to camp, he possessed it only in hope. He was God's pilgrim.

Despite all this, his primitive morality still showed itself in certain respects ungainly and hesitant, and sometimes distinctly sinful. The dominant note in these pages is, nevertheless, religion—a religion which terms God the God of Abraham, meaning the God who called Abraham, made a covenant with him, and asked of him absolute faith, generous hope, and a love born not of flesh and blood, but of God.

Read GENESIS 12:1-9 The call of Abraham
        17   The covenant with Abraham
        22   Abraham's sacrifice

These are the key chapters in the life of Abraham; but since he is a patriarch of such great importance, we recommend reading all the chapters from 12 through 23.

We draw particular attention to the passage on Melchisedech (14:18-20), and the visit of the three angels (chapter 18), followed by Abraham's beautiful prayer in behalf of Sodom.

Here Romans 4:18-22 and Hebrews 11:8-18 (as well as Galatians 3) must be reread; these passages throw a pure light on Abraham's faith.

The promise of the Saviour must be studied in our Lady's Magnificat (Luke 1:46-55); and the promise of innumerable descendants, in the epistle for All Saints' Day (Apocalypse 7:9–10).

✠

Isaac

ISAAC represents the pivotal point, so to speak, in the tradition of the three patriarchs. His marriage was the salient feature of his life. To his father, he was the victim for the holocaust; for his son, he was the unwitting instrument in the transmittal of the messianic blessing to the man of God's choice.

Read GENESIS 24   The marriage of Isaac
        27   The transmittal of the blessing

✠

Jacob

JACOB'S life was full of stirring events. We call attention particularly to his vision of the ladder, and his subsequent consecration of Bethel, the place where the vision occurred. This action is like a sort of remote appeal to that special abiding presence of God which was one day to hallow the Temple. When Jacob returned from his exile in Mesopotamia, an angel wrestled with him in a mysterious contest and changed his name from Jacob to Israel. His twelve sons were to be the heads of the twelve tribes of Israel. Finally, in the great prophetic blessing which he bestowed on his children in his last hour, he pointed to Juda as the one in whose tribe the Saviour would be born.

Christ will be the son of Adam, of the race of Sem and of the tribe of Juda.

Read GENESIS 28:10–22	Jacob's dream and his consecration of Bethel
32	Jacob becomes Israel
49	Jacob imparts his blessing and dies

✠

Now we have met the trinity of patriarchs—Abraham, Isaac, and Jacob—who stand at the threshold of religious history. What is of greatest moment to us in their story is the revelation of God Himself. He is the only true God, whom we must never tire of seeking in the Bible, for man's eternal life is to know the only true God.

Now the God who reveals Himself to us, the living God, the one God, is He who took upon Himself the work of creation, and chose to make a covenant with man; He is the God of Abraham, the God of Isaac, and the God of Jacob.

Our faith recognizes Him and learns God's ways of acting—His divine manners—so that we in our turn may respond to them as we should. These lofty ideas are transmitted to us in a clothing of historical events in which God's designs are disguised and, sometimes, completely concealed; whence comes the sin, the dust, the mire of this earth—the same earth on which the Word of God became incarnate.

☦

TO BRIDGE the gap between the history of the patriarchs and the happenings in Exodus, we have the ingratiating interlude of Joseph. Through his fortunes, God brought about a sudden change in the course of events.

Jacob's children and the other members of his family numbered seventy souls. This small clan was now to become a people. God, by His mysterious providence, meant to send them into a prolonged exile in order to prepare them for their mission. This was the going down into Egypt.

It should be noted how the personal vocation of a man of God has a scope that extends far beyond him as an individual, reaching out to the whole Church and to humanity at large.

Joseph was a just man who forgave his persecutors and became the savior of his fellows; thus in several respects he prefigured Christ.

Read GENESIS 37; 39–48; and 50.

CHAPTER 4

On the Move

✠ ✠ ✠

Exodus

EXODUS is one of the key books of the Old Testament. It tells how the children of Israel were constituted as God's chosen people, and describes their spiritual development. This notion of people of God reveals one of the most important of the divine intentions. It is a prelude to the mystery of the Church and the society of the blessed in heaven.

The people of God, freed from the slavery of Egypt, were now to celebrate the paschal solemnity, cross the Red Sea, and journey through the desert toward the promised land. All this was the doing of the true God. God? God is He who is mindful of His people, and who saves them with His strong hand and His outstretched arm. These truths they will repeat from generation to generation.

The book opens with the account of the call of Moses and the revelation of the divine Name—"I am He who is." It is noteworthy that the Eternal reveals Himself at the same time as the God of Abraham, the God of Isaac, and the God of Jacob, the Lord God of the fathers of the children of Israel.

Read EXODUS 1–5.

Through the hand of Moses, God sent upon Egypt the famous plagues, which clearly show how He forwarded the cause of His people. These events may be read in Exodus, chapters 7 through 11.

The same account recurs in the "wisdom" literature, Wisdom, chapters 16 through 19.

All that God did to free His people hinges on the institution and celebration of the first paschal solemnity and the crossing of the Red Sea.

Read EXODUS 12–15.

This story is related in the form of praise of God in Psalm 104. It must not be forgotten that it really refers to eternal salvation:

> And I saw as it were a sea of glass mingled with fire, and them that had overcome the beast, and his image, and the number of his name, standing on the sea of glass, having the harps of God: and singing the canticle of Moses, the servant of God, and the canticle of the Lamb, saying: "Great and wonderful are Thy works, O Lord God Almighty; just and true are Thy ways, O King of ages. Who shall not fear Thee, O Lord, and magnify Thy name? For

Thou only art holy: for all nations shall come, and shall adore in Thy sight, because Thy judgments are manifest" (Apoc. 15:2–4).

During Holy Week the Church celebrates the sacred mysteries for which the first paschal solemnity was a preparation.

✠

THE MARCH THROUGH THE WILDERNESS

HERE is a new theme of great importance to our own lives. This is the call not of one man, but of an entire people. When God wishes to train a chosen soul, He takes him away from his familiar background and leads him into solitude before He reveals Himself. The Israelites were to be pilgrims for forty painful years in the solitude of the wilderness. All this period was dominated by the events on Sinai, which were the very heart of the Old Testament. God had made a general covenant with Noe, and a personal covenant with Abraham; now He made a covenant with an entire people. The call of this people was expressed in terms that St. Peter later adopted to address the Christian Church.

You shall be to Me a priestly kingdom, and a holy nation (Exod. 19:6).

18

You are a chosen generation, a kingly priesthood, a holy nation, a purchased people: that you may declare His virtues, who hath called you out of darkness into His marvellous light (I Pet. 2:9).

The giving of the law signified the making of the covenant, which was sealed in the blood of the victims offered in sacrifice. God gave the law, and the people promised to keep it; He was to be their God, and they were to be His people; God chose them, and they accepted Him. After Moses had read the law to them, they acclaimed and approved it with a single voice. Then Moses took the blood of the victims and sprinkled it over the altar, the book of the covenant and the people, saying: "This is the blood of the covenant which the Lord hath made with you concerning all these words" (Exod. 24:8).

And taking bread, Jesus gave thanks . . . and gave to them. . . . In like manner the chalice also, after He had supped, saying: "This is the chalice, the New Testament in My blood, which shall be shed for you" (Luke 22:19–20).

Read EXODUS 19 How the covenant was made
20–23 The law
24 The sacrifice of thanksgiving

The absolute part of the law—that is, practically speaking, the Ten Commandments—is contained in Exodus 20:1–21. The Ten Commandments are summed up in the twofold commandment of the love of God and our neighbor (which we find explicitly stated in Deuteronomy 6:5 and Leviticus 19:18).

Luke 10:25–28 should be reread in this connection.

In God's designs, this march through the wilderness had an important part to play in the spiritual development of His people. They were entirely dependent on Him, and—in the interests of the salvation of the human race—separated from all other peoples. The Lord was very near to them, and the tent of the tabernacle was His abiding place in the midst of His own.

The central event of Sinai was preceded and followed by a series of other happenings, some of them particularly important, which formed the setting of this very characteristic period in the life of the people of God.

In Exodus, chapters 15 through 17, we call attention especially to the miracle of the manna—in connection with which John, chapter 6, must be read—and the touching scene of the victory over Amalec.

Exodus, chapters 32 through 34, recounts the apostasy of the people and the worship of the golden calf. Idolatry was a sin against the covenant and against love; for this reason, we shall find that the prophets always referred to it as "adultery." [1]

Chapters 35–40 explain the structure of the tabernacle and tell how it was erected. These chapters are marked by deep religious reverence.

✠

Numbers

LET us go on to the book of Numbers. We call attention in this book to chapters 10:11 to 14:45 inclusive, then chapters 16 and 17, and finally chapters 20 to 24 (in chapter 20 occurs Moses' doubt, and in chapters 22 to 24 Balaam's prophecies). These chapters relate the last events in the march through the wilderness. The forty years of wandering, with their alternate trials and consolations, commandments from God and fresh efforts, served as an education for the whole people.

It must never be forgotten that these people were the people of God. In them the way was being prepared for the Incarnation of Jesus Christ, the Saviour of all men, and for the Christian religion. This preparation was slow and painful, and not without setbacks; but it went on nevertheless surely and tirelessly.

---

[1] A theme of apostasy and idolatry runs through the Bible, for instance: Isaias 44:6–23 and 46 (note the terrible irony); Jeremias 2:1—4:4; 10:1–16; Ezechiel 14:1–11; Apocalypse 13.

When God makes advances toward us, we should receive them with attention and faith,

> For I would not have you ignorant, brethren, that our fathers were all under the cloud, and all passed through the sea. And all in Moses were baptized, in the cloud, and in the sea: and did all eat the same spiritual food, and all drank the same spiritual drink: (and they drank of the spiritual rock that followed them, and the rock was Christ). But with most of them God was not well pleased: for they were overthrown in the desert.
>
> Now these things were done in a figure of us (I Cor. 10:1–6).

✠

Leviticus

LASTLY, to form an idea of the religious training of the people of God, one should read Leviticus, chapters 17 through 22, the Code of holiness. The Church uses some passages from these chapters in the Mass; see, for instance, the Mass for Ember Saturday in September. Here we find that assertion, worthy of the Sermon on the Mount: "Be ye holy, because I the Lord your God am holy" (Lev. 19:2).

✠

Deuteronomy

TO UNDERSTAND the spirit of the life in the desert, and the characteristics of the religion of the chosen people during these years, there is no better way than to read the homiletical part of Deuteronomy (chapters 4–11 and 27–34).

These passages will show us the meaning of the divine laws, the expression of love of God and hope based on the great things He has done in the past: "These words which I command thee this day, shall be in thy heart" (Deut. 6:6).

This last part of the book contains also the great passage of blessings and curses, the confirmation of the covenant, Moses' last canticle and the account of his death.

And there arose no more a prophet in Israel like unto Moses, whom the Lord knew face to face, in all the signs and wonders, which He sent by him, to do in the land of Egypt to Pharao, and to all his servants, and to his whole land, and all the mighty hand, and great miracles, which Moses did before all Israel (Deut. 34:10–12).

✠

THE PROMISED LAND

Josue

THE BOOK of Josue begins by narrating how the chosen people passed over the Jordan. The departure from Egypt and the entrance into the promised land were marked by two miracles of a like nature.

Then came the celebration of the first paschal solemnity in the land of Chanaan. On the following day they ate the products of that country, "and the manna ceased after they ate of the corn of the land" (Josue 5:12). When they crossed the Jordan, they had entered upon a new stage in the designs of God.

This migration of the chosen people makes us think of the continual passage of the souls of the faithful from this vale of tears into the true land of God, where each of them will find a place prepared for him by Jesus in the Father's house (see John 14:1–3).

Read JOSUE 1–5.

THIS reading may well be continued through chapter 11 for a summary of this first conquest (the capture of Jericho, the renewal of the covenant, the battle against the kings, and other events).

As a sacred hymn celebrating these records of great deeds, we may incorporate into our prayer, in all its real perspective, the last psalm of Sunday Vespers—Psalm 113.

It remains to read Josue's last admonition to the people, and the account of his death. The thoughts that filled the souls of these men of God stand out plainly, and it is easy to trace their favorite religious themes.

The remembrance of past benefits is always present, being the pledge of the fulfillment of promises in the future. But the pact of the law regulates the relationships between God and His people. They who observe the law will be blessed, and they who violate it will infallibly be punished.

Read JOSUE 23 and 24.

✠

Judges

THE ENTRANCE of the children of Israel into the promised land meant a great change in their life, not only because the wandering in the desert was at an end, but because of the presence of the Chanaanites. By the time of Josue's death the strength of the Chanaanites had been permanently broken; but numbers of them still survived, and they were both rich and well armed. They held some very important points in the country—Jerusalem, and the length of seacoast inhabited by the Philistines. Israel therefore had to come to terms with them and live in their immediate vicinity, and here lay a great danger for the national and religious life of the people of God. Their "espousals . . . in the desert" (Jer. 2:2) were soon compromised by acts of infidelity; they prostrated themselves at the feet of the local idols and served Baalim and Astaroth. When one or other of the tribes was guilty of apostasy (for each of the tribes of Israel was fully

25

independent at that period, and there was no central power), the Lord let it fall under the yoke of one of its nearby adversaries.

When, however, the trial had lasted long enough, and in its misfortunes the erring tribe had turned back again to the true God, the God of Abraham, the God of Isaac, and the God of Jacob, who sets men free and saves them, He would raise up a liberator. Then the idols were cast away, weapons were taken up again in the name of Yahweh, and liberty was regained. This general theme is clearly set down in one single chapter.

Read JUDGES 2:6—3:6.

Anyone who would like to see a few picturesque and lively examples, may look up

Judges 4 and 5	Debbora and Barac
6–8	Gedeon and Abimelech
10:6–18 and 11	Jephte
13–16	Samson

✠

Samuel

AT THE end and culmination of this whole period, we meet with the pure and saintly personality of Samuel. First we read a touchingly familiar story, how Samuel was born and how God called him; then how an extraordinarily tragic event occurred —the ark of God fell into the hands of the Philis-

26

tines. We must realize what this trial meant to Israel's faith; the ark was the symbol of the presence of the Lord in the midst of His own people. In this hour of combat, they had brought out the ark to make certain of victory. The text shows the religious importance of this act, in the eyes of both the Israelites and the Philistines. The outcome was that Israel suffered a serious defeat, and the sacred ark fell into the hands of God's enemies. Such an incredible disaster as this was unheard of. The Bible tells us how the old high priest Heli met his death as a result of his emotion. "The glory is departed from Israel, because the ark of God was taken" (I Sam. 4:22).

This test of Israel's faith had a happy ending; the true God was glorified, the idols were put to shame, and the return of the ark took the form of a religious procession.

Read I SAMUEL 1–3.

CHAPTER 5

Establishment of the Kingship

✠ ✠ ✠

THE ESTABLISHMENT of the kingship was a
fresh turning point in the history of the people of
God, for it created unity among the separate tribes.
The kingship and the kingdom cast light on the
Messias and his work. The Christ would come to
found the true kingdom which God had always intended to establish. But Samuel, the man of God,
was displeased with the motives that impelled the
people of Israel to ask for a king. The Israelites
wanted to "be like all nations" (I Sam. 8:20). Was
there no risk then that they would lose their strong
sense of their exceptional call? The most remarkable thing in this story is that Samuel, whatever his
personal tastes and his own views, submitted completely to God. Once God told him to establish the
kingship, he did not hesitate one instant.

Read I SAMUEL 8–10.

When Samuel thought the time was ripe, he abdicated his office of judge and officially took leave of the people. On this occasion his one thought was to remind Israel of the great acts by which the true God, the God of their fathers, had manifested Himself. And the people, fickle and changeable as they were, still asked Samuel to pray for them as he retired from the judgeship.

Read I SAMUEL 12.

To give ourselves a little rest, we might pause at this point and read the beautiful eulogy of the fathers of the children of Israel in Ecclesiasticus, chapters 44 through 46.

Then follows the tragic recital of two great faults committed by Saul. Samuel, who had established the kingship against his will, had attached himself to the person of Saul; but now he was obliged to reject him. Great was Samuel's sadness, but his fidelity to the Lord was unwavering and controlled his other feelings.

Read I SAMUEL 13:5–14; 15.

✠

David

SAUL was rejected, and David was chosen. The life-like story of David stands out in the Bible in strong relief. War, poetry, love, and religion, together with sin and repentance, actuated his many-sided personality. Many of the psalms reflect the shifting scenes of his life. He was the head of that house to which Christ would one day belong. We shall first consider his call.

Read I SAMUEL 16.

The thrilling details of David's early life are given in I Samuel 17–26. We call attention particularly to chapter 16 for the battle of the youthful David with Goliath, where his faith appears so transparently; then to chapter 18 for his friendship with Jonathan and his love for Michol; and to chapters 24 and 26 for his magnanimity.

The events of David's wandering and dangerous life were for him so many themes for prayer, as we learn from the psalms (see 53, 55, and 58). They show us David's religion in his hours as a fugitive, and his personal relations with the Lord. But reaching beyond any historical event to which they originally referred, these psalms also serve to express the prayer of the Church. The words of the psalms belong to the Holy Spirit, and He breathes life into them in our souls.

The account of King Saul's rejection is followed by his tragic end, his anguish and courage, his last exploit and his suicide; finally we learn of David's fidelity and the funeral elegy. These accounts should be read in I Samuel 28 and 31, and II Samuel 1.

After a whole series of struggles and wars by which he united the country under his leadership, David succeeded in taking Jerusalem. This stronghold in the mountains of Judea, which had been a rallying point for David's enemies in the very heart of the country, now became the holy city of the people of God. Thither David brought the ark of the covenant amid a solemn religious demonstration.

Read II SAMUEL 6.

Probably it was when David brought the ark into the city that he composed the beautiful Psalm 23, which the Church chants during Advent and on Ascension Day. This is the psalm of the coming of the Lord of glory.

Michol, David's wife, did not understand the religious significance of the joyful entry of the ark into Jerusalem, and David never forgave her.

What did Jerusalem become in the hearts of the people of God? To understand this, we must read the prophets—the plaints of Jeremias in the lamentations which we sing at the Tenebrae services in Holy Week, as well as the triumphal visions in the Book of Consolation, chapters 51:16 to 52:12; 54; 60; and 66:6–14.[1] Here Jesus' entrance into the city should be reread in Luke 19:37–44, and lastly

---

[1] See page 65.

the description of the new Jerusalem in the Apocalypse 21:9–27.

But the outstanding event of David's life, which throws light on all the rest, is the choice God made of his person to be the royal ancestor of Christ. Christ's kingship was foreshadowed and embodied in the messianic promise made to David. God, taking the initiative once again, looked upon His people and made His choice. And knowing this divine choice, we can only marvel at the spontaneity of David's religion.

Read II SAMUEL 7.

From this time onward the kingship of the Messias became one of the hopes of Israel. We find it, for instance, in such prayers as Psalms 88 and 131. Reminding God of His promises, the psalmist feels full of confidence—for how then can he fail to be heard? It is plain that this is no mere formula, but a contact with a Person truly present.

Later the prophets were to constitute themselves the interpreters of these promises. Isaias for example proclaimed:

A Child is born to us, and a Son is given to us, and the government is upon His shoulder: and His name shall be called, Wonderful, Counsellor, God the Mighty, the Father of the world to come, the Prince of Peace. His empire shall be multiplied, and there shall be no end of peace: He shall sit upon the

32

throne of David, and upon his kingdom (Isa. 9:6–7).

The Angel Gabriel announced to Mary the fulfillment of God's royal plan (Luke 1:32), and at the birth of Christ's precursor, Zachary chanted the Benedictus, which throws light on the same mystery (Luke 1:68–79). The Benedictus is one of the New Testament canticles embodied by the Church in her daily Office.

The King of kings and Lord of lords is described last of all in the Apocalypse 19:11–16; and in 22:16 we read the words that give David's kingship its deathless echo: "I Jesus . . . am the root and stock of David."

In the light of these divine promises and this divine choice, not to mention David's natural graces, strength and charm, his sin appears all the more detestable and pitiable. It casts a very harsh light on the fundamental weakness of man, original sin, and the necessity of a Saviour. David was the man according to God's own heart; if David fell, then "he that thinketh himself to stand, let him take heed lest he fall," as St. Paul warns us (I Cor. 10:12).

The king's sin was magnificently atoned for by his touching repentance. He had been blinded by passion, and the sincerity of his penance was complete.

33

In the same connection we must also observe the upright and intrepid personality of the prophet Nathan.

Read II SAMUEL 11 and 12.

Psalm 50, "Have mercy on me, O God," which the Church attributes to King David, has become her classic expression of penance. Psalm 129 may be associated with it, since its prayerful accents bear on the same themes.

All is well. God instantly pardons him who repents; but—and this law is invariable throughout the Old Testament—the sin must still be expiated. Moses was not permitted to enter the promised land; Heli saw disaster overtake Israel; and David must see the child of his sin die, and the sword lifted forever against his house. The wages of sin is death. Christ Himself, taking this heritage upon Him, accepted death willingly. We, His followers, are delivered by His resurrection from the fears of death; but we also must accept death humbly, faithfully, and calmly as an expiation for sin.

The assassination of Amnon the crown prince, Absalom's revolt and death, and Adonias' conspiracy—such were the tragic scenes that marked the king's old age and his life of penance. (The details of this romance are read in II Samuel 13–20 and I Kings 1 and 2:1–12.) The real immediate facts of David's last years may not, of course, be judged outside the framework of his epoch; but to unearth from them the divine spark which never went out beneath the ashes, it is necessary to:

Read II SAMUEL 23:1–7.

✠

The Psalms

DAVID'S life marks a turning point in the Bible; and just here we can well establish a contact with the Book of Psalms, a large number of which are attributed to David. We shall mention only a few, which will suffice as landmarks and first points of contact.

Psalms 147 to 150 inclusive, called by the Jews "Hallel," are psalms of praise. A person first reads these verses to form an idea of the thought they contain; then gradually he comes to use them as a prayer and finds them a powerful help towards spiritual progress.

Psalm 135, which is somewhat similar, is a beautiful type of litany-psalm in honor of Yahweh the God of Israel.

The penitential psalms form a group: Psalms 6, 31, 37, 101, and 142, together with the two Psalms 50 and 129 of which we have already spoken.

The Church has made great use of this series of psalms to voice her repentance and her appeal for God's mercy.

Certain psalms refer more directly to Christ, and are known as the messianic psalms:

Psalm 2, on the Messias King.

Psalm 15, in which the Church finds the prophecy of Christ's resurrection.

Psalm 21, on the just man who suffers persecution. This psalm has a special meaning for us because it contains the verses which Christ recited on the Cross: "O God My God, why hast Thou forsaken Me?"

Psalm 109 speaks of the Messias as King and Priest. It is the first psalm of Sunday Vespers.

To close the list, we give a few very beautiful prayers chosen here and there in the psalter:

Psalm 18: joy in the Lord.

Psalm 22: the good shepherd.

Psalm 26: a prayer of confidence and hope.

Psalm 28: a nature psalm, telling of God in the storm.

Psalm 39: a complete program for one's spiritual life.

Psalm 44: a royal epithalamium or love song.

Psalm 90: one of the most beautiful psalms at Compline.

Prayers in the hour of distress often recur among the psalms, men being so often in distress; there are also many prayers of thanksgiving or praise, and others of petition or hope based on the wonderful works which God had wrought for His people.

Perhaps we have now said enough to open the psalter for our readers and give them the urge to return to it at leisure.

✠

Solomon

"AND Solomon sat upon the throne of his father David, and his kingdom was strengthened exceedingly" (I Kings 2:12). We must pause here at the prayer that Solomon addressed to God asking for the gift of wisdom—a pure and upright prayer that was pleasing to the Lord.

Read I KINGS 3.

The famous story of Solomon's wise judgment is related immediately afterward, and then in chapter 5 we find a short summary of the king's greatness and renown. His sumptuous display made a lasting impression on the oriental imagination. An example of this is the beautiful story of the visit of the queen of Saba in chapter 10.

> The queen of the south shall rise in the judgment with the men of this generation, and shall condemn them: because she came from the ends of the earth to hear the wisdom of Solomon; and behold more than Solomon here! (Luke 11:31).

As an example of this Israelitic wisdom, it would be well to read here a few passages from Proverbs:

37

the exhortation placed in the mouth of wisdom (1:20–33); wisdom and friendship with God (3:1–12); the value of wisdom (3:13–26); and the two passages used by the liturgy—the excellence of wisdom set forth in her own words (8:22–36), and the valiant woman (31:10–31).

The Canticle of Canticles should also be viewed in connection with Solomon.

King Solomon's chief work was the building and dedication of the Temple. The lavish use of gold and the minute care expended on the execution of every detail of the edifice are, be it admitted, characteristic of Solomon's mentality; but they also reveal genuine respect for God. From now on the Israelites had a permanent place of worship. The stark simplicity of the journey through the wilderness had become a thing of the past. Some of the prophets were to show an instinctive mistrust of the Temple; was there no risk that it would engender routine and that the religious rites would become soulless? These were no idle fears, and the men of God kept harking back to the spiritual life led in the desert, when God dwelt under a tent made of skins in the midst of His people, and everything led them to live in His presence and under His sway. Nevertheless, the ceremony and the prayer by which the Temple was dedicated show great religious depth and purity of soul.

This Temple, which would one day be destroyed

and rebuilt, had its forerunner in the tabernacle used in the wilderness (Exod. 25–31). A new Temple was foreseen in vision in Ezechiel 40. But in reality it was neither in the ark nor in Solomon's Temple that God meant to dwell with men. Christ was to say that the Temple is His Body (John 2:19–22 and Mark 14:58), "for in Him dwelleth all the fullness of the Godhead corporeally" (Col. 2:9).

The Christian people are the fullness of this Body:

> Know you not, that you are the temple of God, and that the Spirit of God dwelleth in you? (I Cor. 3:16).

> For you are the temple of the living God; as God saith. . . . (II Cor. 6:16).

> Now therefore you are no more strangers and foreigners; but you are fellow citizens with the saints, and the domestics of God, built upon the foundation of the apostles and prophets, Jesus Christ Himself being the chief corner stone: in whom all the building, being framed together, groweth up into an holy temple in the Lord. In whom you also are built together into an habitation of God in the Spirit (Eph. 2:19–22).

This is the great and beautiful theme of the divine indwelling and the communion of saints inter-

twined in a single mystery. St. Peter likewise takes
it up in his first epistle (I Pet. 2:2–10).

Read I KINGS 5:15—7:51; 8.

The liturgy of this dedication of the Temple conferred on King Solomon an almost priestly role,
and the prayer that he uttered on this occasion is
one of the most beautiful pages in the Old Testament. He was fully aware that consecrating a house
to the name of the Lord was an unprecedented act!

> Is it then to be thought that God should indeed
> dwell upon earth? For if heaven, and the heavens of
> heavens cannot contain Thee, how much less this
> house which I have built? (I Kings 8:27).

But the glory of the Eternal had filled this house
of the Lord, and His name was to be there. The outstanding thought in this prayer is to proclaim once
more God's care for His people and His faithful-
ness. He is a God who forgives and saves His
people, and this is proved by the great deeds He
has wrought in the past. This prayer expresses a
true sense of morality with regard to the question
of sin and likewise great religious sincerity; it also
contains a remarkable passage looking toward a
universal religion (verses 41–43).

So it was that God loved this house and Solomon's dedication of it. He appeared to the king to
make this known to him, reminding him that his

reign would be pleasing or displeasing to God according to his fidelity in observing the divine commandments.

Read I KINGS 9:1–9.

In the passage just cited, the threat of all the deportations and calamities to befall Israel if the people were unfaithful was already clear. Solomon himself, alas! gave the example of evil conduct. The unprecedented splendor of his court may have catered to the pride of his people, but the burden of keeping it up by servitude, labor, and gifts in kind, ended by wearing them out. The greatest evil of all was the foreign wives whose love corroded the king's heart and turned it away from God.

This makes us think of what Christ was to do in restoring to woman her dignity as man's single helper, the position which we saw accorded her in the first three chapters of Genesis.

Read I KINGS 11:1–13.

Solomon's death marked a new turning point in the destiny of God's people and hence in the divine Economy.[1]

To understand more clearly how the law was

---

[1] The history of David and Solomon is also given in I Chronicles 10–29 and II Chronicles 1–9. Here the events are arranged in such a way as to bring out their theological implications.

the pedagogue of the chosen people under the Old Covenant, it would be interesting at this point to go back over Leviticus 8 and 16, and then read immediately afterward Hebrews 7:1—10:18.

In the wisdom literature we find a eulogy of David and Solomon; another eulogy, that of Simon the son of Onias, stresses the significance and grandeur of the priests' duties (Ecclesiasticus 47 and 50).

CHAPTER 6

The Prophets Called by God

✠ ✠ ✠

GOD set apart a long time for the training of His people. He called Abraham, revealed Himself to Isaac and Jacob, delivered the children of Israel from Egypt and led them for forty years across the desert, and at last gave the promised land to the twelve tribes. He raised up David, a man according to His own heart, to be their king, and made them glorious under Solomon; but no sooner was Solomon dead than a schism occurred (what a mystery, that the people of God could have been divided by a schism!). And we call to mind Christ's priestly prayer: "That they may all be one" (John 17:21).

Ten tribes broke away from the house of David, while Juda and Benjamin, holding Jerusalem and the surrounding territory, remained faithful to Solomon's son.

Read I KINGS 12.

From then on there were two kingdoms.

The northern kingdom was that of Israel, which lasted from 931 to 722 B.C. Israel was to have nineteen kings who belonged to nine different dynasties. Although it was the schismatic kingdom, God did not abandon it; and He sent it prophets.

The southern kingdom was that of Juda, from 931 to 586 B.C. It had twenty kings, all of whom belonged to the house of David. A few of these kings were wise, God-fearing men, for instance the devout Ezechias whose history is recounted in II Kings 18 through 20. Several of the others, however, committed all the crimes typical of the pagans, and led their people into idolatry.

God raised up prophets in this kingdom also.

Assyria, the New Empire, the Persians, and the Medes were to succeed one another in the foreground of the political and military scene; the promised land was to be subjugated, and its populations deported. But throughout this era the soul of Israel and Juda was to be developed, purified, and spiritualized by the labors of the various prophets. It is plain that this was a decisive turning point in God's designs for the coming of the Messias.

The people, once they were in possession of the promised land ("inhabitants on the earth," in the phrase of the Apocalypse 17:8), relied too much on themselves. They were in danger of identifying grace with prosperity, and earthly power with the kingdom of God. Now that they were no longer pilgrims, the messianic Hope was frittered away in various hopes of an immediate and everyday nature.

For this reason the men whom God called to become prophets had to be entirely subject to His control, speaking only the words that He gave them to speak. When things seemed to be going well with the people and prosperity reigned, the prophets were commissioned to foretell ruin and war, and often terror and human disaster. In the time of the exile, however, when the people were helpless and on the verge of human despair, these same prophets restored their courage, and reawakened their confidence by reminding them of God's promises and foretelling a future bright with glory and joy.

✠

Elias

THE KINGDOM of Israel was the home of Elias. This prophet lived for God alone. Nothing could corrupt his integrity, intimidate his bold spirit, or make him yield to human pressure; moreover, his powers as a wonder-worker had to be reckoned with. The labors he underwent and the singleheartedness of his devotion to God must be read in the Bible itself.

Read I KINGS 16:29—19:21.

45

Chapter 18 in particular relates the contest between Elias and the pagan priests. The prophet's sheer fidelity and conviction and the terrible shafts of his wit converted the people. At the end of chapter 19, the call of Eliseus shows us how one prophet was anointed by another. In the story of Naboth's vineyard the man of God took a firm stand for social justice.

Read I KINGS 21:1–29.

Elias was mysteriously taken up into heaven, while his spirit passed to Eliseus.

Read II KINGS 2:1–14.

Just as Moses typifies the law in the Old Testament, so Elias typifies the prophets:

> Remember the law of Moses My servant, which I commanded him in Horeb for all Israel, the precepts, and judgments. Behold I will send you Elias the prophet, before the coming of the great and dreadful day of the Lord. And he shall turn the heart of the fathers to the children, and the heart of the children to their fathers: lest I come, and strike the earth with anathema (Mal. 4:4–6).

Now the angel who appeared to the priest Zachary in the beginning of St. Luke's Gospel said to him:

> Fear not, Zachary, for thy prayer is heard; and thy wife Elizabeth shall bear thee a son, and thou shalt

call his name John: and thou shalt have joy and gladness, and many shall rejoice in his nativity. For he shall be great before the Lord; and shall drink no wine nor strong drink: and he shall be filled with the Holy Ghost, even from his mother's womb. And he shall convert many of the children of Israel to the Lord their God.

And he shall go before Him in the spirit and power of Elias; that he may turn the hearts of the fathers unto the children, and the incredulous to the wisdom of the just, to prepare unto the Lord a perfect people (Luke 1:13–17).

Upon Mount Thabor Elias and Moses appeared one on either side of Jesus; and when the disciples came down from the mountain they asked Him, saying:

"Why then do the scribes say that Elias must come first?"

But He answering, said to them: "Elias indeed shall come, and restore all things. But I say to you, that Elias is already come, and they knew him not, but have done unto him whatsoever they had a mind. So also the Son of man shall suffer from them."

Then the disciples understood, that He had spoken to them of John the Baptist (Matt. 17:10–13).

With the era of the prophets, we come to the part of the Old Testament which should perhaps contribute the most to the spiritual development of our souls. The prophets proclaimed the message that God sent to His people, to rebuke them and lead them to return to Him. At the same time, above and beyond any particular words addressed in this way to man, God Himself makes Himself known to us through their medium.

We must therefore read over these utterances of the prophets so that we may hear in them the message which the Holy Spirit will bring to life within us; and so that we may recognize in them God's designs, intentions, and ways, and let our lives be affected by them. They do contain a message for us and a challenge from God. We must familiarize ourselves with these prophetic utterances; then their lines of force will meet and increase in strength until they make an impression on our minds and influence our hearts. Thus we can be constantly turning back to God with ever deepening conviction.

✠

Amos

AMOS was a prophet in the kingdom of Israel in the eighth century B.C. A shepherd and somewhat rough of speech, his principal theme was that of false security which trusted in the outward performance of worship and ritual—literal but soulless. He insisted on social justice, flaying the rich for their luxury and profiteering.

Read AMOS 2:4–16; 4–6; 8:4–14; 9:8–15.

The last-named passage paints in remarkable images the great vision of the restoration to come; it will surely come, because God's love will be victorious in the end.

✠

IN 721 Salmanasar conquered Samaria. He led away the majority of the inhabitants into captivity, and brought pagan populations into the kingdom, where they mingled with what was left of God's people. In exile, some of the Israelites recovered themselves. They looked forward to Him who had been promised to their fathers and in whom all nations would be blessed.

Here it would be well to reread the beautiful canticle of Tobias, which the Church uses in her official prayer every Tuesday at Lauds (Tob. 13).

It may be taken as an example of the theological point of view regarding the exile.

✠

Osee

OSEE was the second prophet belonging to the same era and country. His book must be read in its entirety. Its great themes are God's love for His people, the infidelities of Israel, and, in alternation, predictions of the punishments God will inflict and promises of salvation from Him.

God reveals Himself as a Bridegroom. He makes known to us the love He bears His creature—a poignant love and, if we reflect that He is God, an overwhelming love. He announces His plan: He will allure His people and lead them into the wilderness, and there:

> I will espouse thee to Me for ever;
> and I will espouse thee to Me in justice,
>   and judgment,
> and in mercy, and in commiserations.
> And I will espouse thee to Me in faith:
> and thou shalt know that I am the
>   Lord (Osee 2:19–20).

Texts such as these, which form the heart of Osee's message, reveal a truly interior religion on a high plane of morality and purity. On the other hand, we must see the sins for which God reproached His people—injustice, ritual devoid of soul, and idolatry.

At the beginning of his book, under cover of a parable in action, the prophet makes known a secret hidden in God, namely, that in the creation of the first man and woman, God gave a symbol of His love. On Mount Sinai, God had entered into a covenant with His people, and Israel had pledged

their faith to Him in return. To betray this faith
and worship idols is nothing else than prostitution.

Isaias sounds the same note (54:5–8; 62:4–5),
as does Jeremias (2:2 and 2:20–25; 3; 31:3–7;
31:20–22; and 32). Ezechiel has two powerful chapters of the same character (16 and 23); one passage
in Osee is very impressive (2:14–23).

The Canticle of Canticles should be understood
as having a similar drift, and likewise the royal
epithalamium of Psalm 44.

At length the Bridegroom manifested Himself
in the Gospel. John the Baptist, the forthright
preacher and precursor, conferred on himself the
title of friend of the Bridegroom (John 3:27–30).

Jesus Himself declared in one of His parables:
"A King . . . made a marriage for his son" (Matt.
22:1–14). This is the great reality of the Incarnation.

St. Paul spoke of this same mystery in Ephesians
5:25–32.

Finally St. John showed us its supreme fulfillment in the glorious marriage supper to which all
the elect are called (Apoc. 19:7–9 and 21:1–4).

✠

Isaias

WITH the prophet Isaias we return to the kingdom
of Juda. His book—the most important of all the
prophetic books—is rich in its imagery, powerful

in its utterances and visions, and poignant in many of its passages. It divides itself into two main parts comprising respectively the first thirty-nine chapters and the remaining chapters from the fortieth onwards. The first of these parts evidently refers to the end of the eighth century B.C., and the other was written to comfort the Hebrew exiles after the ruin of Jerusalem.

The Lord the Holy One of Israel will judge His people, and He will make use of pagan nations to inflict punishment on them. But these nations shall be destroyed in their turn, and a "remnant" of the people shall be saved.

In the second part of the book there appears, as it were, a new aspect of the Messias: he will be God's servant and will save his people by his redemptive suffering. Surpassing glory is promised to this people after their deliverance and restoration.

We shall now run through the book in large sections and point out certain key chapters, those which are of deepest religious import and easiest to understand, and therefore most helpful for our first contact.

Read ISAIAS 1.

This vision serves as an introduction to the book. The chosen people had turned away from God. They still worshiped Him outwardly; but what was the value of their religion when they themselves were not holy? Nevertheless, they had at hand a means of cleansing themselves and returning to God:

> If your sins be as scarlet, they shall be made as white as snow: and if they be red as crimson, they shall be white as wool (1:18).

As we read these prophets, an image or sometimes a short verse will echo in our souls like a word coming to us straight from God.

Read ISAIAS 2–5.

The good things that are to come, which are the object of our hope, are interwoven with God's judgments on the actual conduct (and it is always the same story!) of His people. The parable of the vineyard signifies the rejection of His love. This Jewish nation, in the blessings and punishments that befell it, is in all truth the figure of our own relations with God.

Read ISAIAS 6.

Here we find the story of the call of Isaias. It gives us the beautiful trisagion which the Church sings whenever she solemnizes the Sacred Mysteries: "Holy, Holy, Holy, the Lord God of hosts, all the earth is full of His glory" (6:3). This grandiose vision emphasized the role of the angels, and also the absolute fidelity required of a prophet, who must utter only the words that had been spoken to him by God.

Incidentally, Isaias 7:14 is one of the verses that the Church applies to the Blessed Virgin and Christ at Christmas.

Read ISAIAS 9.

This entire chapter deals with the coming of the Messias. The reader will take pleasure in discovering here in their context many cherished verses with which he has long been familiar.

Read ISAIAS 11.

The prophet continued his description of the looked-for king, revealing something of the humanity of Christ. Here we find the list of the gifts of the Holy Spirit as the Church proclaims it when she confers the sacrament of Confirmation. The prophet held out hope that a remnant of the people would be reunited and brought back from exile. The theme of the "remnant" recurs in many of the prophets, and undoubtedly refers to one of God's hidden designs.

These few chapters introduce Isaias' grand spiritual horizons—man's persistence in sin, God's tireless offer of conversion, and the need of firm hope.

The ensuing series of prophecies were directed against the pagan nations. The king of Babylon's descent into hell (Isa. 14:3–23) may be read as an example.

Read ISAIAS 24–27.

These chapters give us a short apocalypse—in other words, a prophetic vision of the end of the world and time. A twofold theme emerges, and we shall meet it again in St. John's Apocalypse: cosmic catastrophe and the terror of the wicked on the one hand, and on the other the song and joy of the men who have been saved by the redemption. This joy is well summed up in this single verse:

> O Lord, we have patiently waited for Thee: Thy name, and Thy remembrance are the desire of the soul (Isa. 26:8).

This hope implies a deep spiritual development.

Read ISAIAS 35.

Following the same trend, chapter 35 of Isaias is one of the most beautiful in his entire message; in fact it is one of the most appealing chapters in the Bible. It describes the return of the Jews from exile, their journey through the desert and joyful entry into Jerusalem; but its significance is far deeper. The true people of God, namely, the faithful who have been saved by Christ, follow after Him as they journey to the heavenly Jerusalem, along the

path traced out by the Gospel, in which even fool:
shall not err:

> Then shall the eyes of the blind be
>   opened,
> and the ears of the deaf shall be unstopped.
> Then shall the lame man leap as a hart,
> and the tongue of the dumb shall be
>   free . . .
> and everlasting joy shall be upon their heads
>   (35:5–6, 10).

This is a mystery where the Old Testament serves
as an image for the New; this one true religion of
"the redeemed of the Lord" (verse 10) belongs to
us even more than to the Israelites, as we see from
Luke 7:12–23.[1]

✠

AT THIS point it would be well to read Micheas, a
contemporary of Isaias. Chapters 1 to 3 treat the
prophetic theme of social justice; chapters 4 and 5,
the hope of a restoration to be effected by the
Messias (Bethlehem is named in verse 2 of chapter
5, and that is why we reread this verse every year at
Christmas); and chapters 6 and 7 contain a very
moving altercation between God and His people.

✠

---

[1] The second part of the Book of Isaias (chapters 40
through 66) will be considered in its logical place after
Ezechiel, under the title of The Book of Consolation, p. 65.

Jeremias

JEREMIAS' prophetic activity was contemporary with the events in II Kings, chapters 22 to 25, in other words with the attempt made by the upright King Josias in favor of religious reform and also with the reigns of the evil kings who succeeded him, and the ruin of Jerusalem under Sedecias. This period covers the years 628 to 587 B.C.

When we read the book, therefore, we must carefully note at what time the various prophecies were uttered (indications are given by the subtitles appearing in the text of the Bible).

We often find very definite bits of information about Jeremias' own life—his call, his difficulties, the ambushes laid for him, and his prayer to God. His work throws light on his whole personality.

Here is a brief summary of the development of the book. The people had turned to idols, and were no longer in good faith; they were offering empty sacrifices, devoid of meaning. For this they were soon to be punished by a foreign invasion. The outcome depended on whether or not they would repent. This people was God's people, and their history had a sacred significance. Hence they were face to face not with mere moral retribution, or the interplay of natural forces; the Lord loved this people whom He had chosen and guided, and now it was He Himself who raised His hand over them. It was a matter of direct relationship between God and His own. In this sense, God's doings have an ever-actual significance; and this is just as true for us as for the Israelites.

Read JEREMIAS 1.

Jeremias' call entailed a cleansing, as was the case with the call of Isaias. This was indispensable for a man who was to be the bearer of God's words. The chapter ends on a note of touching encouragement.

Read JEREMIAS 3.

The apostasy of God's people (the two sisters, Israel and Juda) is presented in a blunt adjuration. This love drama reveals God's yearning over His people, and His extraordinary fondness for them:

> I have remembered thee, pitying thy youth,
> and the love of thy espousals,
> when thou followedst Me in the desert . . .

> Return, O rebellious Israel . . .
> for I am holy, saith the Lord,
> and I will not be angry for ever
>   (Jer. 2:2; 3:12).

Read JEREMIAS 4-6.

The punishment of foreign invasion was now at hand; corruption had gone too far. Nevertheless, appeals for repentance still alternated with the prophecies of impending catastrophe. It was needful that the people be disquieted about the sins which the Lord detested. All this is expressed in concrete and speaking images.

The same theme recurs in Jeremias, chapters 7 through 12. The religion of the true God consists in justice. Sacrifices should bespeak a nation that harkens to God.

Was not Jesus to say the same thing in the Sermon on the Mount (Matt., chapters 5 through 7), and in His denunciation of the hypocritical Pharisees (Matt. 23)?

Chapter 10 of Jeremias speaks again of God's horror of idols, and chapter 11 reminds the people of the covenant.

Jeremias 18:1–17 makes use of the parable of the potter to voice the pathetic complaint of the Lord against His people. The allegory of the potter's vessel reappears in chapter 19:1–13.

Jeremias 23:9–40 apostrophizes the false prophets: "I did not send prophets, yet they ran: I have not spoken to them yet they prophesied" (Jer. 23:21). That a man should be a prophet does not depend on his own initiative; he must receive a call from God, and must heed it with true supernatural fidelity to the very end.

Read JEREMIAS 30–33.

These three chapters form a fitting close for our reading of Jeremias. They bring us back to wide horizons of hope, joy, and divine tenderness—the return of Israel, the new covenant, and the restoration to be effected by the Messias.

Finally we should read the Lamentations of Jeremias. The Church sings these lamentations as a nostalgic prayer, plaintive and yet hopeful, at the Tenebrae services in Holy Week.

✠

Ezechiel

THE DEPORTEES in Babylon did not lead an absolutely intolerable life; they even enjoyed a degree of autonomy. The best of them, however, kept their souls turned toward the promised land. How could they serve God in a strange country? Psalm 136 describes this state of mind:

> Upon the rivers of Babylon,
> there we sat and wept:
> when we remembered Sion . . .
> How shall we sing the song of the Lord
> in a strange land?
> If I forget thee, O Jerusalem,
> let my right hand be forgotten!
> Let my tongue cleave to my jaws,
> if I do not remember thee . . . (verses
>   1 and 4–6).

Some of the Israelites, nevertheless, settled down to make the best of the situation. Tempted by the splendor of Babylonian idolatry, they failed to understand the lesson they should have learned from events, and said, "What is the use?"

Then in the land of exile God raised up the prophet Ezechiel.

Read EZECHIEL 1.

To our way of thinking, the divine vision related in this chapter seems very involved. Its purpose was to remind the exiles of God's transcendency and mystery. We should also notice how the prophet constantly resorts to approximations or comparisons as a means of expressing the ineffable. St. John later spoke in the same way in his apocalypse.

Read EZECHIEL 2 and 3.

These verses are of great interest because they give an idea of the program to which the prophet was called, or, in a broader sense, to which every man of God was called. They emphasize the role of the Spirit, the envoy's complete dependence on the words given him by God, and the fidelity required of him in transmitting them. The missionary had nothing to impart but God's words and all God's words. He had no human message emanating from himself. He must absorb the Word of God and then recount it faithfully to his brethren.

Often the prophet was led to do symbolic deeds, which we call parables in action (for example, Ezechiel 3:22-27 or 12:1-16). Our Lord Himself later did something of the sort when He cursed the barren fig tree (Matt. 21:18–22).

The theme of the false prophets (which we have already met in Jeremias 22:9–40) reappears in chapters 21:1 through 14:11.

Finally, the theme of the vine is elaborated in chapters 15 and 19:10–14. (Note: It is found also in Osee 10:1; Isaias 5:1–7; and Jeremias 2:21.)

Read EZECHIEL 16.

This is the allegory of God the Bridegroom. In this passage the nuptial theme borrows some rather strong images, but we should take them reverently in the sense in which they are intended. They are the medium through which are revealed to us the designs of God's love for His people, and those of Christ's love for the Church and for the souls of each and every one of us, who so often scoff at Him.

Read EZECHIEL 18.

This chapter deals with the question of personal morality. Every man must bear the responsibility for his own acts. These lines amount to a theological treatise on the sinner, his freedom, and God's mercy. It is well summed up in this final apostrophe:

> Why will you die, O house of Israel? For I desire not the death of him that dieth, saith the Lord God, return ye and live (18:31–32).

Read EZECHIEL 23.

Here is a fresh nuptial allegory of the same style as that in chapter 16. The two sisters who have defiled themselves by their sins are the countries of Samaria and Jerusalem.

Ezechiel 24:15–24 contains another parable in action. The lives of these prophets were in God's hands, social conventions and their own feelings being left far behind. It is easy to understand that, humanly speaking, they should have dreaded the prophetic call. Once God had made them the instruments of His zeal for His kingdom, nothing else mattered. But this very service of the kingdom made the grandeur and worth of these men in His sight.

Ezechiel 26 and 27 depict in extremely vivid images the fall of the king of Tyre. These chapters should be compared with chapter 18:1–20 in the Apocalypse.

Ezechiel 31 relates the allegory of the cedar.

Read EZECHIEL 34.

The parable of the good shepherd is a truly Biblical image which often recurs in the writings of the prophets. Here Ezechiel is heralding Christ, who will be the true Shepherd and a descendant of David.

Jesus took up the image and applied it to Himself in John 10:1–18 and Mark 14:27.

We must not try to push this figure too far, but make use of it to lift our minds to the spiritual reality which it both hides and reveals.

Read EZECHIEL 36.

This is perhaps the most important chapter in Ezechiel, because for one thing it proclaims that the people of Israel will be cleansed and dwell once more in freedom in their own land. Still more noteworthy, however, is the theological significance of the passage from verse 16 through verse 37. Sanctification is wrought by God; it is He who takes the initiative and carries out the work. Yet He makes men freely consent to allow Him to act. This is His peculiar glory. "For," writes St. Irenaeus, "it is God's glory that man is a living being." [2] Only God Himself is powerful enough to cleanse us in reality, taking away the stony heart out of our flesh and giving us His Spirit.

Read EZECHIEL 37.

The vision of the dry bones (the seventh prophecy on Holy Saturday) is a powerful proclamation of the communication of new life that was to come. It was a magnificent promise, given to nourish Israel's hope.

From chapter 40 to the end of the book, Ezechiel

---

[2] St. Irenaeus, *Contra Haer.* IV, 20, 7.

foretells the renewal of the kingdom, the Temple, the altar, and the sacrifices.

✠

The Book of Consolation

UNDER this title we present the second part of the Book of Isaias (chapters 40 through 66).

These prophecies, written to reanimate the hope of the exiles, are the most religious and the most "Christian" in the whole Old Testament. Even though it was the hour of tribulation, they seemed to be full to overflowing with the sap of supernatural glory and joy. With the characteristic name of "the islands" and the "ends of the earth," the summons to a universal religion returns more and more plainly. The note of pure and heartfelt religion brings out the wholly gratuitous transcendency of God's actions, and reminds one of the first epistle of St. John.

We should read these chapters in their entirety; for if we have faith, the Holy Spirit will be ready at one verse or another to enlighten our souls and set them on fire with love, as a spark kindles dry twigs.

Here are some examples of the burning words that strew the entire book:

> Fear not, for I am with thee:
> turn not aside, for I am thy God:

I have strengthened thee, and
    have helped thee,
and the right hand of My just one
    hath upheld thee (41:10).

I am, I am He that blot out thy iniquities for My own sake, and I will not remember thy sins (43:25).

I have even called thee by thy name: I have made a likeness of thee, and thou hast not known Me. . . . There is no God besides Me (45:4–5).

And thou shalt know that I am the Lord, for they shall not be confounded that wait for Him (49:23).

O that Thou wouldst rend the heavens, and wouldst come down (64:1).

We have all fallen as a leaf,
    and our iniquities, like the wind,
        have taken us away. . . .
Thou hast hid Thy face from us,
    and hast crushed us in the hand of
        our iniquity (64:6–7).

As one whom the mother caresseth, so will I comfort you (66:13).

We must cut short this list of examples; the only difficulty lies in selecting them.

The various chapters of the book hinge upon two great themes: the deliverance of the people from captivity, to the glory of the new Jerusalem; and the mystery of the Servant of Yahweh.

Here the footnotes in our Bible will prove extremely useful. For instance let us notice the words in chapter 40:3-5, which John the Baptist was to repeat in Matt. 3:3 and Luke 3:4-6; chapter 61, containing the passage chosen by our Lord to introduce His first sermon at Nazareth; chapter 45:8, which is sung by the Church in the Rorate Caeli; and lastly the resemblance between the fall of Babylon in chapter 47 and the ruin of Rome in Apocalypse 17.

As to the mystery of the new Jerusalem and the Church, we point out especially chapters 54 and 60, the latter of which is so comforting and so full of glory that the Church repeats it every year in the liturgy of Epiphany. Chapters 62 and 66 draw the picture of what the Church will one day become.

To conclude, certain songs contained in the Book of Consolation, concerning the Servant of Yahweh —that is, Jesus Christ, strike a note of truly poignant tenderness and clarity. The first of these songs, in 42:1-7 and 49:1-7, relate to the call and mission of Christ; the other two, in 50:4-9 and 52:13 through 53:12, preach the gospel of the Saviour's passion, death, and triumph. In these passages the book perhaps attains the loftiest prophetic heights of the entire Bible.

✠

ALTHOUGH the three short books of Tobias, Judith, and Esther are of later composition, they might be read at this point.

Literary beauty and great depth of thought will be discovered also in the three chapters of Jonas. This book is remarkable in that it expresses a call to a universal religion, for God loved Ninive too, and forgave it when its people did penance.

CHAPTER 7

Home to Jerusalem

✠ ✠ ✠

IN THE richest of imagery the prophets had foretold the return of a "remnant" of Israel to the promised land.

In 539 B.C. Cyrus—who, as the Bible gives us to understand, was an instrument in God's hand—promulgated an edict that permitted the Jews to return to their own country and rebuild the Temple. In actual fact it was only a frail remnant who made their way back to the promised land. When these men reached home they found their land occupied, and were obliged to live under wretched conditions. The faith of new prophets, however, buoyed up the people's hope, and the energy of leaders providentially raised up, kept them "separated" so that they remained pure and free to carry out their essential mission.

Slow and laborious this return was, and beset with many obstacles and obscurities. Nevertheless, for the best among the exiles it was a joy beyond their farthest dreams; and it was a decisive step towards the advent of the Messias King.

Psalms 78 and 79 still bring us the echo of the prayers the Israelites had addressed to God while they were captives in a foreign land.

✠

Esdras

Read ESDRAS 1 and 3.

THESE chapters report the proclamation of Cyrus by which the children of Israel were set free, the building of the altar of holocaust, and the laying of the foundations of the new Temple. Some of the people wept and others shouted for joy. To understand the deep significance of this era, we must bear in mind that the people were attached to the promised land by the call they had received from God. Jerusalem, moreover, was His city and the Temple His house, the mysterious place of His presence in the midst of His own.

All this now found a new beginning. The people had regained their mission, their call, their kingdom, and their God.

The two chapters of the little book of the prophet Aggeus fit in at this point. The Temple must be rebuilt before the Israelites' own houses, said Aggeus, for it would be filled with a mysterious glory.

The first two chapters of Zacharias speak of the

need for conversion and give a glorious picture of the new Jerusalem. Chapter 8 proclaims God's love for Sion and His great designs for it.

Malachias alludes to the universal sacrifice in chapter 1:11, and in 3:1 foretells the mission of Jesus' precursor.

✠

Nehemias

Read NEHEMIAS 1–5.

MORE than half a century after the first return to Jerusalem, we come upon the winning personality of Nehemias. While he was cupbearer to King Artaxerxes at Susa, he learned of the misery of his brethren and felt himself called to go to their aid. He received permission to set out. On his arrival he met with immediate opposition, but his faith was tremendous. While the Israelites rebuilt the walls of Jerusalem with one hand, they were obliged to defend themselves with the other. Thanks to Nehemias a moral purification took place among the foremost of the people. His own disinterestedness was unimpeachable.

Read NEHEMIAS 8–10; 12:27–43.

The people solemnly renewed their covenant with God. The story of this great religious renewal is one of the very beautiful pages of the Old Testament. The rite of renewal was performed according to the words of the law—God's words. The people's hearts were touched; and this reminds us how, on the day of Pentecost when the multitude had heard Peter's sermon

They had compunction in their heart, and said to Peter, and to the rest of the apostles: "What shall we do, men and brethren?" (Acts 2:37).

Here we have a living instance of the power of God's word to convert souls. The sacred history of God and His people, telling how He had revealed and pledged Himself to them, was here recited as a creed, a hymn of praise, and a motive for hope (Nehemias 9). By the use of these verses we can easily live this event over again and take part in it ourselves in prayer.

So religion once more took its place in the lives of a "remnant" of the people, now that they had come back and reinstated themselves in the land of God. But how, this time, were they to retain the spirit of the desert—that spirit of complete liberty of soul and constant progress towards God? The answer to this question was found in the practice of religious pilgrimages. Annual pilgrimages had taken shape even before the days of the kings,[1] and now they were revived. There are not a few instances in the Bible where certain rites or deeds are

---

[1] I Sam. 1:3.

enjoined as a means of acquiring some particular spiritual attitude. So the Israelite was commanded to leave his house and his village or city to go and present himself in the Temple on the three great feasts of the year.

The first of these feasts was the Pasch, which celebrated the going forth from Egypt and the covenant in the desert. No one must forget that the Jews had eaten the paschal lamb standing, with their loins girt, shoes on their feet and staves in their hands, and in haste—for it was the Passage of the Lord (Exod. 12:11). Was there any doubt, then, that they were a pilgrim people?

The second was Pentecost, which commemorated the covenant of Sinai in the midst of the desert. In this place and by this solemn pact God had promised to be with His people, and the people had promised to obey all God's commandments.

The third was the feast of Tabernacles, which was kept in remembrance of the wanderings in the desert, and also in thanksgiving for the harvest and petition for rain. This feast lasted for a week, during which the pilgrims remained at Jerusalem, living in bowers made of branches.

Thus the law was the pedagogue of the chosen people, leading them to regard themselves as but wayfarers on this earth and to judge of all things accordingly. In the Book of Psalms we find a whole

73

group of pilgrim psalms, the *Songs of Ascents* or *Gradual Psalms*. They are among the richest in love, hope, and joy.

Here are a few examples:

Psalm 83, whose spiritual meaning is crystal clear. As I made my way to Jerusalem, my heart and my flesh rejoiced in the living God. The nearer I came, the more my strength increased. I have chosen to remain on the threshold of God's house, rather than to dwell in the tent of sinners.

Psalm 125, which gives a good idea of the psychology of the "remnant" who returned.

Psalms 121; 131; and 132.

While we are thinking about this period of Israel's life, we might make a contact with the "wisdom" literature dating from after the exile.

Job we have already spoken of. It is a book of amazing literary beauty and great importance.

Its principal thesis, an answer to the problem of suffering befalling the good, is that man must view himself in true perspective, that is, as a creature. If he cannot understand even the outward world, how is he to probe into God's hidden designs? So let him leave matters to God, adore His wisdom, and trust in Him whatever the ordinances of the divine Will may be (Job 38 to 41).

Ecclesiastes is a little disconcerting to us but its influence has not been negligible, for it has shown men that their minds are not everything, and has

74

wakened within them a secret nostalgia for the world beyond. One commentator has called this book "inspired pessimism." As an example, chapters 1:1–11 and 11:7—12:8 may be read.

Ecclesiasticus, so called because the Church made great use of it in the beginnings of Christianity, is pre-eminently a book for moral training and religious education. One may read, for instance (in addition to the passages already cited in the present work), chapters 1 and 2 (noting particularly the great beauty of the first six verses of chapter 2) and the whole of chapter 24, in which occurs the eulogy of Wisdom set in Wisdom's own mouth.

The last of the series, the Book of Wisdom, is closely akin to the New Testament. We suggest that chapters 1 through 3:9, and 4:7–20, be read. A sense of future resurrection and retribution is already clearly marked; chapter 9 contains Solomon's prayer; and chapters 13 through 15 set forth the religious and philosophic thought of the wise.

CHAPTER 8

The Last Witnesses

✠ ✠ ✠

TO ROUND out our Old Testament reading, we shall select a few passages from Machabees, and then turn to the book of Daniel, which will bring us to the border line of the New Covenant.

Alexander the Great made an end of the Persian Empire, and the promised land fell under Hellenic domination. Due to various combinations of circumstances, the inhabitants of Jerusalem were now to be massacred anew, the walls of the city destroyed, and a fortress surmounting Mount Sion occupied by a Syrian garrison. Before long the practice of religion would be forbidden under pain of death. Finally the "abomination of desolation" foretold by the prophet Daniel (Dan. 9:27) would be seen when sacrifices were offered on the altar of holocaust to Jupiter Olympius.

Had God deserted His people?

✠

Machabees

Read II MACHABEES 6 and 7.

HERE we read of the example given by these devout Jews who were ready to lay down their lives in witness to their faith. They are the martyrs of the Old Testament.

The saintly old man Eleazar declared at the moment of his death that his soul was well content to suffer for fear of the Lord. The death of the seven brethren and their mother is an admirable lesson in faith and hope, and affirms the resurrection of the dead.

Read I MACHABEES 1:1—3:9.

Passive resistance gave place to a holy war, which in turn won for the Jews a short period of independence.

✠

Daniel

THE PROPHET Daniel brings us to the great apocalypse of the Old Testament.

The first part of the book is chiefly concerned with the story of the three young Hebrews at the court of King Nabuchodonosor, who were valiant enough to refuse to yield to an order to commit idolatry. The narrative is followed by the celebrated Canticle of the Three Children, calling upon all created things to bless God, which the Church

77

recommends for our thanksgiving after Communion.

Read DANIEL 3.

The second part of the book reveals, in mysterious imagery, hidden things which will come to pass at the end of time. Just as John's apocalypse was to be a message of comfort and supernatural hope for the first Christians in the days of persecution, so Daniel's apocalypse with its vision of God's victory was a source of mighty encouragement to the Jewish people during the persecution of Antiochus Epiphanes.

Read DANIEL 7.

The four beasts signify the four empires that dominated the land of God after the exile—the Chaldeans, the Medes and Persians, the Greeks, and finally the persecutor Antiochus Epiphanes himself, who profaned the Temple. But to crown all the woes and sins of men there came the abomination of desolation; then Daniel was given a stupendous vision of the Ancient of Days (God) and the mysterious Son of man. The books were opened, for it was the hour of judgment, the hour of the kingdom of God.

The passage in chapter 7 consisting of verses 9 through 14 is particularly meaningful. In verses 13–14 appears for the first time the messianic title by which Christ was to refer to Himself throughout His public life. (See Matt. 24:30, and particularly 26:64–65; Acts 7:56; and Apoc. 1:13.)

Chapter 9 of the Book of Daniel relates the prophecy of the seventy weeks.

The prophets sought, says St. Peter, to discover what times and circumstances were indicated by the Spirit of Christ who was in them; for the Spirit foretold the sufferings that Christ was to endure and the glory that was to follow His sufferings (I Pet. 1:10–12).

In his prayer Daniel rehearses the memory of God's great benefits, which are the firmest ground for confidence with regard to the future (9:4–19).

Chapters 10 and 11 of the Book of Daniel reveal Israel's sufferings and persecutions.

Read DANIEL 12.

The angels hold a very special place in the Book of Daniel (just as they do in John's eschatology).[1] Michael, their prince, foretells the deliverance of the people, and beyond and above that—for his words open up more distant and significant horizons—the last judgment and eternal retribution.

✠

---

[1] Eschatology is the doctrine of the last things—death, heaven, hell, judgment, and the second coming of Christ.—*Translator's note.*

IN THE year 40 B.C. Herod, a foreigner, was proclaimed king of Judea by the power of the Roman Senate. The scepter had been taken away from Juda, according to the ancient prophecy made by Jacob before his death. All had been fulfilled.

A few years later, an angel of the Lord appeared to a priest of the class of Abia named Zachary, while he was performing his sacred functions in the Temple.

God, the true God, the living God, created the world. He chose Abraham. He delivered His people from Egypt, led them through the Red Sea, made a covenant with them in the desert, brought them into the promised land and divided it among them. He chose a king—David. When His people were unfaithful, He scattered them and purified them; He raised up prophets for them, and brought back a remnant of them. He fulfilled all the promises.

Son of Adam, of the race of Sem, descended from Abraham, of the tribe of Juda, of the house of David, the Saviour of the world might now come.

Reread PSALM 88.

It was time to ask the Virgin Mary's consent:

> And the Word was made flesh,
> and dwelt among us (John 1:14).

The Gospel According to St. Matthew

✠ ✠ ✠

NOW that we have familiarized ourselves with God's communications under the Old Covenant, and especially with the message of the prophets, we shall have a new approach to the words of Christ.

Let us take St. Matthew. This Gospel was the one most used by the primitive Church for the instruction of her catechumens; it is also the one that most directly connects the New Testament with the Old.

The evangelist keeps himself in the background, and stresses particularly the sermons delivered by Jesus. It is easy to see that Matthew is repeating living phrases, cherished in his memory—or rather in his heart—for his style is that of the spoken word. The balance and repetition of phrases and images are characteristic: "You have heard that it was said to them of old. . . . But I say to you"; "Blessed are they. . . . Blessed are ye"; "A wise

man that built his house upon a rock. . . . A foolish man that built his house upon the sand"; "Lay
not up to yourselves treasures on earth. . . . But
lay up to yourselves treasures in heaven," and so on.

Christ is the one who speaks and we hear Him—
He is addressing us. We should make up our minds,
be converted, and rejoice in the good tidings.

Behold the strange King, the son of David, the
son of Abraham, fleeing into Egypt and dying at
Jerusalem. Behold finally the Lamb for the holocaust; behold the Temple destroyed and rebuilt in
three days. Behold the Lord even of the Sabbath,
Him who fulfills the law and the prophets. Behold
Him who was looked for and who came in the
name of the Lord, the beloved Son in whom the
Father was well pleased. Behold the Son of man
who will be seen coming in the clouds of heaven in
great power and majesty.

> Jesus went about all Galilee, teaching in their
> synagogues, and preaching the Gospel of the King-
> dom: and healing all manner of sickness and every
> infirmity, among the people (Matt. 4:23).

Now the promise had given way to the fulfillment. The kingdom had begun—but how unlike it
was to the popular expectations of it! It was devoid
of glory and earthly power, for God's kingdom is a

kingdom of saints. The Magna Charta of its citizenry is the Sermon on the Mount.

Read MATTHEW 5–7.

Although this kingdom really begins here on earth, it is still the object of our faith and hope. Jesus revealed its mysterious growth to us in the parable chapter.

Read MATTHEW 13.

The interior religion inculcated in the Sermon on the Mount is radically opposed to a spiritual attitude which Christ detests. We must reread with very close attention and in its bearing on our own lives the discourse our Lord addressed to the hypocritical scribes and Pharisees.

Read MATTHEW 23.

In conclusion, the prophet Daniel's entire eschatological message is taken up again by our Lord in His description of the second coming and the last judgment.

Read MATTHEW 24 and 25.

To find out how much Matthew depends on the Old Testament, we have only to run our finger along the footnotes in his Gospel and observe the constant references to the books of the prophets—

Isaias, Osee, Jeremias, Micheas, Daniel, and Zacharias—and to Genesis, Exodus, Leviticus, Deuteronomy, Samuel, the Books of Kings, Chronicles, and especially the Psalms.

✠

The Gospel According to St. Mark

THE NEXT time we decide to go through the Bible, we must take up at this point the Gospel of St. Mark. Mark was a disciple of St. Peter, and acted as his interpreter at Rome. Careless of literary style yet with a wealth of picturesque details, he faithfully noted down the Apostle's sermons. This last fact is what gives interest to his message.

This very short Gospel can easily be read at one sitting. The main divisions are as follows:

Introduction (1:1-13).

Jesus' preaching tour in Galilee (1:14—8:26).

The turning point of the public life—St. Peter's confession of faith at Caesarea Philippi (8:27-39) and the Transfiguration (chapter 9).

The journey through Perea to Jerusalem, during which Christ particularly applied Himself to training His disciples (chapters 10-13).

The Passion and Resurrection (chapters 14-16).

Mark is given to description. It has been pointed out, for instance, that he almost never reports an important speech made by Jesus without mentioning His lively glance. In the material presented by the four Gospels, the passages peculiar to Mark are as follows:

Jesus' relatives endeavor to lay hold on Him (3:20–21).

The parable of the seed that sprang up of itself (4:26–29).

The cure of a deaf mute (7:31–37).

A blind man is given sight, at Bethsaida (8:22–26).

A young man flees, casting off his garment, at the time of Jesus' arrest in the garden of Olives (14:51–52).

CHAPTER 10

The Acts of the Apostles

✠ ✠ ✠

THIS book has also been called the Gospel of the Holy Spirit. It begins with Pentecost. All things had been made ready and had been fulfilled by Christ in His own Person; now all things must be imparted to His bride, the Church.

The Church? It is Jesus Christ glorious, imparted and diffused by the Holy Spirit. The book of the Acts describes the amazing new way of life of the first Christians. It tells of the singular graces bestowed on the primitive communities at Jerusalem and Antioch and on the churches founded by Paul along the shores of the Mediterranean. It informs us how, after Christ's ascension, the Holy Spirit reigned in a manifest way over all the faithful. Here we read of the charisms, trials, joys, constant prayer, and generous testimony of the members of this kingdom of God, in the fullness of time.

It bears the stamp of its author, St. Luke, and reveals its kinship with the third Gospel.

All this exuberance of life which sprang immediately from Pentecost remains the ideal towards which the Church has instinctively turned in every age.

Read ACTS 1–12.

We call attention to the following points:

The primitive idyll of Jerusalem in two short passages (Acts 2:40–47 and 4:32–35).

One of the most beautiful quotations from the prophet Joel (Acts 2:17–21).

St. Stephen (Acts 6 and 7).

The "acts of Peter" (Acts 9:31—11:18).

The second part of the book is completely dominated by the personality of the Apostle Paul. St. Luke reports for us Paul's great missionary journeys, his manner and his determined stand at the Council of Jerusalem to maintain the freedom of the new Christians from the Old Law. These chapters, which cover the period during which Paul wrote to the churches, should be used as the background for a chronological study of the composition of his epistles. We should begin, however, by reading the book of the Acts in its entirety. This book is of fundamental importance to the Church, and every Catholic should have a firsthand knowledge of it from beginning to end.

Read ACTS 13–28.

CHAPTER 11

Letters by the Apostles

✠ ✠ ✠

WE SHALL take up the epistles in the order in which they were written, following the main divisions of St. Paul's life. We intend to point out in each epistle the subjects that are easiest to understand at a first reading.

✠

THE GREAT ESCHATOLOGICAL THEMES

Thessalonians

IN OUR first division of Paul's life, we come upon his two epistles to the Thessalonians. Here St. Paul picked up the themes of St. Matthew and Daniel relating to the last things.

He had founded the church of Thessalonica on his second missionary journey (Acts 17), and wrote to its members from Corinth. The first epistle begins by showering praise on these recent converts of his:

Read I THESSALONIANS 1:1–10.

Then Paul reminds them of how he had founded their community a short while back, sent Timothy to help them, and rejoiced in the good report Timothy had sent him. Paul's familiar and lively tone bears evidence of the very close ties between him and his communities. These letters with all their forthrightness show the conviction of Paul's religion. He opens out to his readers undreamed-of horizons, and conveys to them all the freshness of the Gospel message.

Read I THESSALONIANS 2 and 3.

After a brief exhortation to sanctity of life, Paul comes to a serious question. What of the end of this world, and, more immediately, what of death? The first converts gave themselves joyously to the good tidings. Just as the Lord had gone up into heaven on the day of His ascension, so He would return in His second coming to judge the living and the dead, and inaugurate His glorious kingdom. But these events were slow in taking place, and by now some of the Christians were already dead. What would become of them? He repeats the command of the Gospel that Christians must watch, adding a few words as to how the resurrection of the dead will come to pass.

Read I THESSALONIANS 4 and 5.

This epistle might be compared with Jesus' own teaching. It will be seen that the images of the clouds of heaven, the thief in the night, and of the pains of childbirth recur here.

In his second epistle St. Paul touches on the mystery of Antichrist. He thanks God that He has chosen the Thessalonians for salvation and called them by Paul's preaching, and urges them not to waste their lives in idle waiting but to make ready, and this with generosity, for the final coming of the Lord.

Read II THESSALONIANS 2 and 3.

Notice in 3:14–15 the tone of fatherly reprimand and the evident expectation that his advice will be taken to heart. Repeated examples of this same spirit are to be found throughout Paul's epistles.

✠

The Epistles of Peter

AT THIS point we will interrupt Paul's letters in order to read St. Peter's two epistles, which follow a line of thought similar to that of the epistles to the Thessalonians.

The first of these two letters (addressed to a fairly large group of Christian communities) is remarkable for the way in which it orientates the whole spiritual life of the Church toward the coming of her Lord. This precious message must never be allowed to fall into oblivion, for it gives us an idea of what our own love for Christ should be. All the members of the Church on earth are wayfarers, and St. Peter shows in a very realistic way, though always in the light of supernatural hope, the circumstances under which the Church ordinarily exists. It is normal, he warns us, and therefore no matter for surprise, that the Church should undergo suffering, persecution, and trials; yet at the same time, to the eyes of faith, she is ever resplendent with glory, fervor, and love.

The Spirit has begun the work of the resurrection in us. Christ is the cornerstone, and we also are living stones; the living spiritual temple is in process of being built up.

It is fundamental that we are called to be saints, and Peter lays down the conditions of sanctity—humility, obedience, reverence, and courage. (Note these virtues: how is that we sometimes allude to them as "natural"?)

How can we pass over a text like this:

> Sanctify the Lord Christ in your hearts, being always ready to satisfy everyone that asketh you a reason of that hope which is in you. But with modesty and fear (I Pet. 3:15–16).

Does not this give us a glimpse of the apologetics of the primitive Church?

The joy of this epistle is pure, unadulterated, and

strictly evangelical. The general underlying thought, which not infrequently becomes explicit, is that of the brevity of life. It is noteworthy that the eucharistic prayer in the Didache (the book of the doctrine of the twelve apostles, belonging to the beginning of the second century) closes with this invocation: "May Grace come, and this world pass away!" [1]

The Second Epistle of St. Peter comes back to the theme of eschatology. The glorious return of the Lord Jesus is certain, although its exact hour is unknown. The same images recur here which we have already noted in the Gospels and the First Epistle to the Thessalonians; notice, moreover, that at the close of this book St. Peter alludes to the epistles of "our most dear brother Paul" (II Pet. 3:15–16).

The short epistle of St. Jude might be read at this point.

✠

ST. PAUL AMONG THE GREEKS

Epistles to the Corinthians

PAUL was at Ephesus (Acts 19) when he was told of certain grave disorders having broken out in the community he had founded at Corinth. Besides, this church had referred to him several questions about particular problems, which it behooved him to answer.

---

[1] *The Didache,* trans. James A. Kleist, S.J. (Westminster, Newman Press, 1948), p. 21.

We may take this opportunity to observe the life of these first Christians. Many aspects of it were most attractive, but the cockle sown by the enemy and the scandal of sin had already made their appearance. These things had been predicted in the Gospel; and among the twelve who lived so close to the Lord for three years, there had been a Judas.

In the First Epistle to the Corinthians, we call attention to the following points:

Chapter 2, on true wisdom, made known by the Spirit who searches the deep things of God.

Chapter 11:18–33, on the institution of the Holy Eucharist. This testimony is of the greatest importance for us. Verses 26 through 29 show the meaning of real faith in this mystery, and the spiritual nature of the act of Holy Communion.

In chapter 13, the Pauline hymn of charity.

In chapter 15, the clearest words in all Scripture on the mystery of the resurrection. The basis of Paul's doctrine is the first Easter. Because of Christ's resurrection, the body of each and every faithful Christian, being sown in corruption,

> shall rise in incorruption. It is sown in dishonor, it shall rise in glory. It is sown in weakness, it shall rise in power. It is sown a natural body, it shall rise a spiritual body (I Corinthians 15:42–44).

We notice how Paul's thought has developed and gained in precision since the epistles to the Thessalonians.

In the Second Epistle to the Corinthians St. Paul speaks at length of himself, in order to refute certain baseless charges made against him. He proudly gives an apology for the Christian ministry (chapters 3 through 7), organizes a collection for Jerusalem (8 and 9), and lastly gives his own personal apologia (10 through 12). This is a valuable source of information on Paul's background, interior life, and apostolic adventures.

The last verse of this epistle (13:13) contains the most beautiful Trinitarian doxology (tribute of praise) in the whole Bible.

✠

GREAT THEOLOGICAL CONTROVERSIES

Romans

NOW we come to St. Paul's great theological controversies.

It was from the city of Corinth that Paul sent his letter to the Romans. The church at Rome had been founded by other Christians and already enjoyed a great reputation. Paul intended to visit it, and took due precautions beforehand against the Judaizers (persons who wished to make the observances of Judaism binding on Christians).

The fundamental, principal, and indispensable contact with God is that of *faith*. Our Lord and

Saviour Jesus Christ reveals God to us and justifies us. The Gospel alone is the source of all sanctity.

> The Gospel . . . is the power of God unto salvation to every one that believeth. . . .
> For the justice of God is revealed therein, from faith (Rom. 1:16–17).

In the second section of his letter, St. Paul sets forth the effects of justification by faith. This section interests us most of all. It stresses the role of the Holy Spirit in a most enlightening way, speaks of the divine sonship of adoption, hope in the resurrection, and love of Christ here and now. These themes are rich with all the amplitude of the Christian's new life.

Read ROMANS 5–8.

Chapters 9 through 11 deal particularly with Israel's special problem—the call of the Jews, their rejection, and their conversion at the end of time.

The same problem is set forth in the Epistle to the Galatians, particularly 3:25—4:7.

✠

THE EPISTLES OF THE CAPTIVITY

IN THE course of his two years' captivity in Rome, Paul had time to think out and write his two great Christological epistles, the letter to Philemon and

the letter to the Philippians. These broad horizons
of St. Paul's complete the revelation of the mystery
of Christ and the Church.

✠

Ephesians

THE FIRST two chapters of this epistle present one
of the most powerful syntheses of our Christian
faith.

They begin by setting forth God's eternal plan,
in which the Father, the Son, and the Holy Spirit
concur in the work common to all Three Divine
Persons. Our call comes from the Father, who wills
that we should be holy. Redemption comes from
Christ, through His blood. Sanctification is the work
of the Holy Spirit, who is already given to us as the
pledge of our inheritance of glory.

This plan God accomplishes in the Church, the
mystery of which St. Paul connects with the glory of
the risen Christ.

Read EPHESIANS 1:3–14 and 15–23.

The conclusion of this imposing Christian vision
is set forth in Ephesians 2:19–22.

Paul, the prisoner of Christ, is the apostle of this
mystery; and he prays that those whom he addresses
may be able to comprehend the infinite charity of
Christ and the fullness of God.

96

This epistle should be read in its entirety. The moral part follows directly from the dogmatic part.

✠

Colossians

THE EPISTLE to the Colossians sounds the same note as that to the Ephesians. We call particular attention to the close-wrought passage on the Person and work of Jesus Christ. Another significant chapter is the one which is read in part at the Mass of Holy Saturday; it amounts to a program for Christians who have put on the new man in the light of Easter:

Read COLOSSIANS 1:15–23; 3.

✠

Philippians

IN THIS letter Paul was writing to friends who were particularly dear to him; its tone is simple, open, and joyful. It dates from the time when he was looking forward to a speedy release from his captivity. The Gospel was being furthered everywhere, and Paul's love for the Lord Jesus was torn between two desires—to live in order to labor and merit the more, and to die in order to be with Christ.

He gives a very poignant summary of the mystery of Christ's humiliation and glory:

Read PHILIPPIANS 2:5–11.

Then he returns to the main idea he had treated in the Epistle to the Romans, but this time on a more familiar note. For the love of Christ, Paul had suffered the loss of all things, that he might know the power of His resurrection and the fellowship of His sufferings. This summarizes Paul's attitude towards his own Judaism.

Read PHILIPPIANS 3.

The atmosphere of this letter radiates supernatural joy.

✠

WE HAVE not yet considered Paul's "pastoral epistles" (I and II Timothy and Titus) and the missive to Philemon. The notes in the Bible make them easy to read.

We have already suggested the reading of two long passages from the Epistle to the Hebrews; now we can review its main divisions. It explains to the Christian converts of Palestine that the new and very sober Christian worship is incomparably above the Jewish worship, the Jewish being only provisional, and extols the priesthood and sacrifice of the New Covenant.

The Epistle of St. James remains to be mentioned. St. James was the bishop of Jerusalem; he was a cousin of Jesus. He took a leading part in the first council, the account of which has come down to us in the Acts; his speech in that assembly (Acts 15:13–21) made a sensation.

In his epistle James is concerned with the Christian who has been already justified by his faith in Christ. He shows that this living faith finds a concrete expression in the works of mercy. The spirit of his epistle reflects that of the Sermon on the Mount.

Notice how James, like Paul and Peter, is always turning in hope towards the Lord's coming. Take, for instance, the figure of the husbandman (James 5:7–8).

The allusion to the sacrament of Extreme Unction occurs in this epistle (5:14–15).

CHAPTER 12

The Writings of John the Evangelist

✠   ✠   ✠

TO COMPLETE this contact with the entire Bible, we must now, as it were, scale the highest peak by a consideration of the work of St. John.

St. John's life was a long one. He had lived through the first flowering of Christian life in the communities founded by Christ's apostles. His message is addressed to Christians as wayfarers here on earth, but he brightens their way with a light from on high.

Christ, in His Easter glory and the mystery of His triumphant ascension, is the Lord of the Church. Already we are living by His life, by the Spirit He has sent us. He is the Vine and we are the branches.

This life brings us fellowship with God, victory in Jesus, and the joy He promised us; and we live this life in this world by loving one another, keeping the commandments, and awaiting the glorious coming of the Saviour.

This last coming sustains the Church and urges her forward in her hope.

Read the First Epistle of St. John.

The truly Johannine tone of this epistle is set in the opening passage, which we have already quoted at the very beginning of this book.[1] It is plain that the Apostle is enthralled by the incredible tidings of the Word of Life who has appeared and brings us the fullness of joy through fellowship with God.

"In you . . . the darkness is passed, and the true light now shineth," he writes (2:8).

We are sinners, but Jesus came to take away our sins.

We have known love by this, that Christ gave His life for us; we also should give our lives for our brethren. And John makes a practical application of this love for our brethren which might well bear the signature of James himself (I John 3:17–18).

Then follows an explanation of theological love: love comes first from God, being His gratuitous gift, and in its strength we love our brethren (4:7–21).

✠

ST. JOHN'S GOSPEL

ORIGEN says at the beginning of his commentary on St. John:

―――――――――

[1] Pp. 1–2.

There are four Gospels, which are, so to speak, the foundation of the faith of the Church. The first fruit among them is John's Gospel. None of the others shows the divinity of Christ so completely. So let us make bold to declare it again—the Gospels are the first fruits of all the Scriptures, and among the Gospels the first fruit is John's. No one can understand it unless he has leaned on Jesus' bosom, and from Jesus received Mary to be his Mother.

We shall start with the passage which we read at the end of every Mass:

Read ST. JOHN's Prologue.

Here John leads us into the very bosom of the Trinity at the moment of the creation of the world, and carries us on to the incarnation of Christ: "And the Word was made flesh, and dwelt among us" (John 1:14). The humanity of Jesus, therefore, was from the first instant taken up into the Person of the only Son of God.

It would be interesting to turn back to the Book of Proverbs 8:22–36; that of Ecclesiasticus 24:1–22; and that of Wisdom 9, to discover the first outlines of the personification of Wisdom in the Old Testament.

St. John's concrete details are very precise, his chronological and geographical setting very accurate, and his presentation very lifelike. Take, for instance, the account of the man born blind (John 9).

The miracles in his Gospel have been deliberately selected to lead us to the heart of divine mysteries. They are "signs," and Christ's discourses on each of these occasions instruct us as to their meaning for our faith.

The multiplication of the loaves introduces the discourse on the bread of life (John 6).

The man born blind supports our Lord's assertion: "I am the Light of the world" (John 9).

The resurrection of Lazarus proves Christ's declaration: "I am the resurrection and the life" (John 11).

We come in contact with the power of these revelations if we receive them with faith in the miracle by which they are expressed.

The dramatic unfolding of the story of the light might be traced throughout this Gospel. The light was offered to the world, and the surrounding darkness became even blacker until it seemed to have extinguished it; but at that very moment the light triumphed, as we are reminded in the liturgy of Holy Week when the light reappears from behind the altar where it has been entombed.

If John's Gospel is the divinest part of the whole Bible, the discourse after the Last Supper is the divinest part of John's Gospel.

Read JOHN 13–17.

Here we have entered the holy of holies of theology, in other words, the secret of God's inmost life, that of the Three Divine Persons.

This is eternal life: that they may know Thee, the only true God, and Jesus Christ, whom Thou hast sent (17:3).

I have made known Thy name to them . . . ; that the love wherewith Thou hast loved Me, may be in them, and I in them (17:26).

The Holy Ghost, whom the Father will send in My name, He will teach you all things, and bring all things to your mind, whatsoever I shall have said to you (14:26).

In that day you shall know, that I am in My Father, and you in Me, and I in you (14:20).

These things I have spoken to you, that My joy may be in you, and your joy may be filled (15:11).

At the end of the Gospel, two very lifelike chapters (20 and 21) depict for us the days of Christ's risen life.

✠

ST. JOHN'S APOCALYPSE

WE STILL have to establish a contact with the Apocalypse, the message addressed by the Lord Jesus from the beyond of His resurrection to His

Church on earth. This message crowns the eschatologies of Paul, Peter, Matthew, Daniel, Isaias, and several other prophets.

Christ, in His glory, is very near to His Church. She must not wonder at being a "partner in tribulation, and in the kingdom, and patience in Christ Jesus" (Apoc. 1:9).

In the very first chapter this triumphant and uncompromising cry is heard:

> I am . . . alive, and was dead, and behold I am living for ever and ever, and have the keys of death and of hell (1:18).

After the Prologue, the seven letters to the angels of the seven churches in Asia make known to us the things that are dear to Christ, among which are patience and truth.

Read APOCALYPSE 1–3.

Then comes a vision of heaven presented in two panels. In the first we are shown God and His court; in the second, the enthronement of Christ. The imagery, whose religious message is not very hard to grasp, has clear theological implications.

Read APOCALYPSE 4 and 5.

There are some other chapters that can be understood without much preliminary explanation:
The epistle of All Saints' Day, which shows the

multitude of the elect standing in the last days about the throne of God and of the Lamb (Apoc. 7).

The last judgment (11:15–19).

The great sign of the glorious woman, clothed with the sun, crowned with stars and the moon under her feet. This refers to Christ's Church, already glorious but still undergoing the devil's assaults and fleeing into the wilderness. According to the interplay between the mystery of the Church and that of our Lady, which is the general rule in the liturgy, this vision also alludes to the Blessed Virgin (chapter 12).

One beast came up out of the earth and another out of the sea, which the devil used to make war with the saints and endeavor to seduce them. But only they "that dwell upon the earth" consented to adore the beasts, and in contrast to their act of idolatry we witness "the patience and the faith of the saints" (13:8, 10).

The Lamb and the virgins (14:1–5).

Rome—Babylon the great—which is to be thrown down. This sign was of great importance for the first Christians, since Rome in their day was the power waging persecution on the infant Church. The extraordinary fall of Rome was to be the first in the long series, for destruction will infallibly overtake every human power that is hostile to the kingdom of God (chapter 17).

THE WRITINGS OF JOHN THE EVANGELIST

The conclusion of this mighty and comforting vision (18:1—19:10).

One of the most glorious visions of Christ (19:11–16). Note particularly His garment and His name (verse 13).

The last judgment (20:11–15).

Last of all comes the marriage of Christ and the Church. Here are a new heaven and a new earth, a new Adam, a new Eve, a new people of God, and a new holy city—the new Jerusalem coming down out of heaven.

Read APOCALYPSE 21 and 22.

Now we have a better understanding of the concluding dialogue (22:17, 20) and that promise on which the Church's whole life depends and whose fulfillment she awaits in loving expectation:

And the Spirit and the Bride say: "Come." . . .
"Surely I come quickly."
Amen! Come, Lord Jesus!

CHAPTER 13

Keeping Up the Contact

☒ ☩ ☒

WE HAVE opened the Bible; let us not close it
again.

The reading of Holy Scripture in the spirit of
faith is a discovery—an eager and reverent discovery of God; it is a contemplation of God. It is
also a dialogue in which He takes the lead and
summons us. We answer, as did all the men of
God, "Here am I,"—and prayer begins to take
shape.

As we turn from reading to prayer and from
prayer to reading, our souls receive light. They are
kindled with love, generosity, faith, hope, and joy,
and transformed from glory to glory into the image
of our Lord Jesus Christ.

We should maintain great liberty of spirit during
this reading of Scripture, and let ourselves be guided
by whatever most attracts our souls. Love implies
preference, and familiarity with the sacred pages

will arouse these preferences in us, and incline us to a certain choice under the guidance of the Holy Spirit. Through the whole maze of books we must often come back to the ones that mean the most to us; and, in each of these books, to the verses that best bring us into contact with the Lord.

To prevent our spiritual life from becoming one-sided, however, we must keep our souls open to the divine proceedings in all their length and breadth. As the Church guides us steadily every year through the various books of the Bible, let us pause to read now one, now another, so as not to lose sight of the whole mystery of Christ.

To Him be "benediction, and honor, and glory, and power, for ever and ever" (Apoc. 5:13). Amen!

INDEX TO
Biblical References
Numerals refer to pages in this volume.

THE OLD TESTAMENT

THE NEW TESTAMENT

INDEX TO BIBLICAL REFERENCES